W. H. (William Hurrell) Mallock

The old Order changes

Vol. III

W. H. (William Hurrell) Mallock

The old Order changes
Vol. III

ISBN/EAN: 9783337051136

Printed in Europe, USA, Canada, Australia, Japan

Cover: Foto ©ninafisch / pixelio.de

More available books at **www.hansebooks.com**

THE OLD ORDER CHANGES

A Novel

BY

W. H. MALLOCK

AUTHOR OF 'IS LIFE WORTH LIVING?' 'SOCIAL EQUALITY' ETC.

'Cette importune économie politique se glisse partout et se mêle à tout, et je crois vraiment que c'est elle qui a dit, *nihil humani a me alienum puto*'—BASTIAT

IN THREE VOLUMES
VOL. III.

LONDON
RICHARD BENTLEY & SON, NEW BURLINGTON STREET
Publishers in Ordinary to Her Majesty the Queen
1886

All rights reserved

BOOK IV.

CHAPTER I.

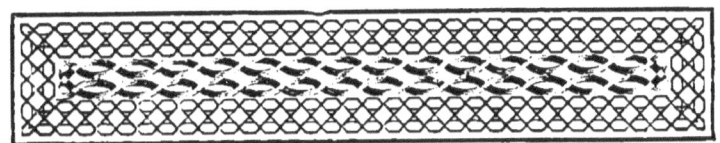AREW was heir to estates in the West of England, a part of which at least had been in his family since the Conquest. There had been hardly a reign in which one of his name or more had not figured prominently in the stirring history of the county—from the days of fighting to the days of borough-mongering: and Otterton Hall, which would one day be his home, had no country house to rival it within a radius of twenty miles.

In addition to these prospects he was in present possession of an income which, for a bachelor, was, to say the least of it, ample. He was able without extravagance to entertain as he had done at the château.

Still, his position was not one of independence. His father, who had been dead for many years, was the second of three brothers; and on his mother, who was still living, had been settled for life nearly all that his father left—a moderate competence. His two uncles, who were still living also, were both of them very old men; and to the estates of the eldest Carew's succession was assured. These estates, however, were much encumbered. The fact was so notorious that many would-be country gentlemen were counting on the day when they would have the chance of bidding for them; and it was at all events hardly open to doubt that unless Carew had considerable means besides, he would never be able to hold his own at the Hall. But his younger uncle, Mr. Horace Carew—a successful dandy of the palmiest days of dandyism, had married a great heiress, who had died leaving no children; and all her fortune, which was quite at his own disposal, he let it be understood was designed for Carew, his nephew. But this was not all. He had not been content with promises. He had practically charged himself with Carew's entire education. He had first sent him to Eton, and then to Oxford; and had since made him an allowance of fifteen hundred a year.

Carew's whole prospects thus hung on this uncle's favour—not merely his prospects of wealth and luxury, but the prospect, far nearer his heart, of restoring the fortunes of his family, and indeed of retaining his old family home.

As for luxury, he was as careless of that as most men; and in his present position he could have made himself quite happy on half or even a third of the income he actually enjoyed. But considering himself in the light of the prospective head of his family, he regarded wealth in a very different spirit. It became in his eye a something which naturally ought to belong to him. It was as much in the fitness of things that he should be possessed of it some day, that he should be surrounded by servants, and eat his dinner off plate, as it was that every man should be possessed of a suit of clothes. Such pomp and circumstance was for him a sign merely; and beyond securing him this, the possession of wealth meant to him the saving an institution with which his whole life was connected as closely as any Hamadryad was ever connected with her oak tree. That institution was his own family; and the preservation and restoration of it was as much an act of piety, to him, as the embellishment and care of an altar might be to a congregation of the faithful. Nor was this feeling on his part mere personal vanity or selfishness. Indeed, when comparing his own family with others, he was extremely modest and sober in his estimate of its comparative importance. He respected it mainly for the sake of the great social principle, of which it was but one amongst many more prominent representatives; and his own prejudices and principles had become more and more stringent, in proportion as those of such other representatives seemed to him to be growing more lax and lukewarm.

This being the case, it is easy to conjecture the feelings with which he received at the château the following information from his lawyer—an old man who was not his lawyer only, but a family friend as well. The letter, indeed, which conveyed it, though enclosed in a blue envelope, was friendly and not official. It began by reminding Carew how the younger of his two uncles had expressed strong wishes as to his making a suitable marriage; and how twice, on conceiving that these wishes might be thwarted, he had shown symptoms of no doubtful anger.

'I quite feel,' the letter went on, 'how difficult and delicate a subject this is to touch upon, but, since I must touch upon it, it is best to speak quite plainly. Your uncle, Mr. Horace, as, of course, you are aware, has the whole of his fortune entirely under his own control, and you can hardly be in doubt as to the result threatened, in case you should contract an alliance which would seriously offend him.

'Well, Mr. Carew, you will forgive my recalling to you how alarmed he was some eighteen months ago by some gossip—some foolish gossip—which reached his ears, connecting your name with that of the Countess de Saint Valery. One can easily understand and excuse an old man's anxieties, looking at the world from the distance of infirmity and seclusion; and he was, as you know, much disturbed by the idea that just at the time when you should be thinking of marriage, you were making your marriage impossible by an entanglement with a married woman— or a woman who, if divorced, would be even more distasteful to him.

'Madame de Saint Valery's subsequent adventures set his mind at rest. He became quite persuaded that your relations with her were not what he had supposed they were. Sometimes, however, it happens that an idea which seems to be dead is really only sleeping, and, I am sorry to say, such has been the case here. Madame de Saint Valery has been at Nice lately, so your uncle hears. He hears, also, that your old intimacy with her has been resumed, and that you have—— It is needless, however, to repeat details. It will be enough to tell you the result. He is persuaded—he has got it into his head, and nothing will get it out—that, since this lady is certainly divorced now, there is a danger—a probability—of your wishing to marry her. On what grounds he bases this fear, who have been his informants, and what they have informed him of, I cannot pretend to say; nor does it concern us now, especially as, you will allow me to add, I disbelieve the entire story. All I have to tell you is this. Your uncle talked over the whole matter with me. No one, as you know, is more obstinate than he is; but no one, though he may do a disagreeable thing, more dislikes saying a disagreeable word. He is therefore determined, come what may, to have no personal dispute with yourself; and he has accordingly requested me, as a friend, not as a lawyer, to convey to you a determination he has arrived at. He hopes that the knowledge of it may influence your future conduct.

'He is going to make an important alteration in his will. I need not now trouble you with the legal details of it; but its practical effect, so far as regards yourself, will be as follows: his fortune, to which he still wishes you to succeed, is, with the exception of one thousand a year, to cease to be yours in the event of your marrying an alien.

'I have now discharged my mission.

'I need only add that, so far as the Countess de Saint Valery is concerned, I do not for a moment believe that this arrangement can have any concern for you; but there are circumstances which may very probably arise, under which you might find yourself seriously hampered by its consequences. For every reason, therefore, it is quite right that you should know of it; and if you should be able to set Mr. Horace's mind at rest, by writing yourself to him and contradicting the reports about you, you would be doing not only a kind, but also a prudent action.

'He is in very feeble health; and his extreme anxiety to have this alteration in his will effected without delay, makes me suspect that, though his doctors speak smooth things to him, he thinks his condition far less certain than they do.'

Carew's first emotion on reading this letter was simply one of bewilderment. As to his uncle's displeasure with him on account of Madame de Saint Valery—of that, it is true, he retained the liveliest recollection. It was the only occasion, during the whole of his life, on which that uncle had addressed him otherwise than with complacency. He recollected the old man's looks, and the very words employed by him. They were these:

'There has been a folly of this kind in the family once before. One of your grandfather's brothers, as you know, ran off with one of these d——d women—monstrous pretty she was, too, so I am told—shot the husband in a duel, and by-and-by married her. He was the eldest son, but, fortunately, it was possible to disinherit him. Now mind this—don't let me hear that you are up to any tricks of that kind. I'm not giving you a sermon on morals—I leave morals to the parson. I speak to you as a man of the world, and as a relation who has some right to speak to you. And in these two capacities I say two things to you—two things, mind : Don't be a fool, and don't disgrace your family. I may add, as a friend, don't ruin your prospects and make yourself miserable for life. Remember what I have said ; and now we'll change the subject.'

Carew did remember. The event was too odd for him to have forgotten it; but not only had the elopement of Madame de Saint Valery opened—at least he imagined so—his uncle's eyes to the truth, and cured him for ever of his suspicions, but Lord Stonehouse, who knew the whole facts of the case, had shown him in the clearest way that there had never been good cause for them. Thus Carew's present astonishment, though the whole communication astonished him, was not due to the nature of his uncle's suspicion, but to the sudden and inexplicable revival of it.

Presently, however, a light began to dawn on him. Mrs. Harley's letter came back to his mind; and he recollected that, in connection with Miss Consuelo Burton's departure, she had mentioned Mr. Inigo as being somehow concerned in the mischief. He now began to put two and two together. Mr. Inigo had caught him on the Promenade des Anglais by moonlight, engaged in a manner that was, without doubt, equivocal; and Carew, with impatient and indignant anger, jumped at the conclusion that the Miss Burtons and his uncle alike had been prejudiced against him by the gossip of this blundering tattler.

In his uncle's case this seemed specially probable, as Mr. Inigo was one of his most industrious parasites. The only question was, what could have been the man's motive ? For crediting Mr. Inigo with all the ambitious stupidity which the largest Christian charity could possibly claim as a shield for him, it was difficult not to believe, in the present case, that his sedulous misrepresentations must have had in them an element of malice.

Anger and speculation, however, of this kind, soon gave way to thoughts that were far more practical. It flashed on him suddenly that, so far as he understood her parentage, Miss Capel was an alien quite as much as her cousin; and the threatened alteration in his uncle's will, if it ruined his prospects in the event of his marrying the one, would be equally fatal in the event of his marrying the other. Miss Capel, it is true, had spoken of herself as an heiress; but with regard to money matters she knew little more than a child; and he had learnt accidentally, from something said by her mother, that the utmost she would inherit from the General would be some six hundred a year.

He rapidly realised the situation. Either he must persuade his uncle that his fears were groundless, and that the proposed alteration in his will was a needless and unfair precaution; or else, for his own part, the matter resolved itself into this: he must choose between Miss Capel (if he could win her) on the one hand, and his hopes of restoring his family, indeed of saving it from ruin, on the other.

In his then mood of mind he could bring himself to renounce neither; and without tormenting himself prematurely by placing these two in the balance, it at once occurred to him that, if he saw his uncle immediately, he might secure an arrangement by which neither would be shut out from him. His action was prompt. It is true that his lawyer's letter had been unopened for two days; but from the moment of his reading it not a single hour had elapsed before he was making preparations for an immediate return to England.

Such, then, were the circumstances of his journey; and it will now be sufficiently apparent what were the thoughts by which his mind was distracted—the problems that lay before him, and the memories that lay behind him, as the clanking train on its long journey northwards was hurrying him away from the land of flowers and sunshine. He crossed from Calais at night; a raw coldness was in the air, and all his future was somehow expressed to his imagination in the bleared lights of Dover revealing themselves through the drizzling mist.

CHAPTER II.

 FEW hours later he woke up from a sleep born rather of dejection than of fatigue, in which he had wandered back to the green pine forests of the Esterels, and had almost arrested the retreating figure of Miss Capel. He brushed away the moisture that was darkening the windows of the railway carriage ; with heavy eyes he peered out into the dimness ; and there, sweeping past him, were the squalid bricks of London, mildewed with morning frost.

A few minutes more, and he was in the echoing gloom of the terminus. A familiar vision of milk-cans, of four-wheeled cabs, groups of shivering porters, and the placards of last night's papers, slowly moved before him, and at last came to a standstill. Then he recognised his servant waiting for him; and he was presently on his way to his own chambers in Curzon Street.

The unchanged aspect of London, as it stared at him through the win'ry morning, struck sadly and strangely on him. His life during his absence abroad had seemed full of hope and suggestion; and now he felt as if that had all gone for nothing, and he had drifted back to the point from which he had started. He could almost believe that the puddles at the gates of the station were the same that his cab had splashed in, on the day of his leaving England. Only one thing struck him as new in any way; and even this made nothing but a very faint impression on him. It was the recurrence on the newspaper placards of words in large type, such as 'Riots,' 'Outrages,' and 'Renewed Alarms,' which he concluded must have reference to affairs in Ireland, or perhaps in Paris. But he gave the matter very little attention; and presently, in a mood of tired disconsolate apathy, he was ascending the stairs that led to his own rooms.

The cloth was laid for breakfast, a bright fire was burning, and a smell arose from somewhere suggestive of chops and coffee; but in spite of these signs of welcome everything looked dismal. There was none of that little daily litter which links us with our surroundings, and makes them seem to sympathise with us. There was nothing to connect the scene with his present self, except two objects—one a copy of that morning's *Times*; the other, a solitary letter lying between his knife and fork. It was a letter from his lawyer, whom he had informed of his movements by telegraph; and the moment he read it, his plans were again changed.

His uncle's house was in Berkeley Square; and it had been his intention, as soon as the hour would permit of it, to report himself at once to the relation on whose action so much depended. Carew was a man who, if people thought him wrong, was generally too proud or too indolent to care to put himself in the right; and when first his relations with Madame de Saint Valery had been misunderstood, he had let the world, and his uncle too, make what they could or what they would out of the matter. But now he had resolved that in his uncle's mind, at least, no shadow of suspicion should be left resting on him. In approaching the subject at all he would have to use much diplomacy; and still more in proceeding to the restrictions that it was threatened would be placed upon his marriage. He knew all this. It would be an affair not of delicacy only, but of time. He had resolved accordingly to lose no moment in beginning.

His lawyer's letter, however, which was but a few lines, informed him that the new will, containing the obnoxious provision, had been actually made already, though it was probably not yet signed; and then followed the news that his uncle, who had been suffering much from the fogs, had left London yesterday, and was now with the Squire at Otterton.

Carew and both his uncles had always been on excellent terms; nor, so far as his personal reception was concerned, was the present unpleasantness at all likely to interrupt them. As for the Squire, he had been an invalid for years, and had never gone farther than the study next his bedroom, or worn any more ceremonious garment than a red velvet dressing-gown. His near relations were his continual guests, and one at a time he would occasionally give them an audience. Often, however, they might be in the house for weeks, and though he would send them a succession of civil messages, they would never receive a single summons to the presence chamber. It thus happened that Carew saw him but seldom; and when he did see him, the interviews were but brief. But at Otterton he was always welcome; rooms were always kept for him there, and he was free to come and go as if it were his own home.

His plans now were accordingly made with promptness. He arranged to go to Otterton himself, that night. He would reach it by midnight, if he left London at five.

By-and-by, after he had had a bath and had breakfasted, and tried in vain to sleep a headache off in a chair, he walked round to Berkeley Square, to hear more detailed news about Mr. Horace. As he stood waiting for the bell to be answered, other thoughts rose in him than those connected with the invalid; and almost for the first time since the beginning of his journey, he began to realize why that journey had been undertaken. His actions, hitherto, had resembled those of a somnambulist, except that the waking with him was a gradual process.

The house, which was designed in a sedate, quasi-classical style, and dated from the middle of the last century, had never been altered since, and looked as if it had never been cleaned. The corroded iron of its railings and its torch-extinguishers, the darkness that lay like a bloom on its chiselled stonework, made its façade seem to Carew like a magic mirror, which showed the square alive with chariots and running footmen, followed presently by the dandies and the statesmen of the Regency—all the signs of that old aristocratic life, when Mayfair was the stately centre of England. It was a house that had been built by his great-great-grandfather; but forty years ago the Squire had been obliged to sell it, and it was only saved from passing out of the family by its present possessor buying it, when he providentially married his heiress.

Carew, as he looked at it, felt his old sense re-awakening in him, that he was connected, as if by fibres which were part of his own being, not only with the people and things which affected himself personally, but with an entire social and an entire political order. He experienced what may be described as a certain expansion of his consciousness, and a half-formed comparison flickered across his mind between the claims of his own position, and the value of a girl's blue eyes.

Presently the door was opened by an old housekeeper, whose face lit up with delight the moment she saw Carew. But directly after, it settled itself into a querulous gravity:

she informed him that her master was really in a very critical condition; and that bad as London no doubt was for him, the journey on which he had ventured was, in her opinion, worse.

Carew turned away with a gathering anxiety in his mind, and, completely absorbed in his own thoughts, walked slowly down to one of his clubs, which was in St. James's Street. He had not yet looked at a newspaper. The *Times* in his own room he had impatiently pushed aside; and he meant now to make up for his negligence. But when, sitting down, he seized on a *Morning Post*, he found he could get no farther than the Births and Marriages. The effects of his journey, combining with his mental depression, rapidly began to tell on him. His eyelids felt heavy; the paper dropped from his hand; the bars of the windows seemed to flicker before him; and leaning back he fell into an untimely doze.

He slept lightly, however, and a sound before long roused him, though he was far too listless to open his aching eyes. He gradually realized what the sound was. It was the sound of a man's voice, who, to judge by his utterances, was evidently talking for the benefit of the room at large.

'Of course,' he was saying, 'this sort of thing is intolerable. Did you hear what happened?—they pulled Lady Harriet out of her carriage; and by their insults they caused such a shock to her nerves, that she actually had to get her sister to receive for her at her fancy ball. I wonder you weren't there. You oughtn't to have missed it.'

'No,' said a second voice, 'I was out of town—I was at Lord Bayswater's.'

'Lord who?' said the first voice. 'Why don't you call him Robertson? I,' it continued, with a magnificent haughty weariness, 'can't really keep pace with all of these new peers.'

Carew felt a smile spreading itself over his lazy lips. Without looking, he had recognised Mr. Inigo. But his smile, though one of amusement, was by no means one of complacency; and, could he have done so unnoticed, he would have walked out of the room. Unable to do that, he lay back still in his chair. He hoped, being in a shady corner, that he might escape Mr. Inigo's observation, and he was doing his best to fall asleep again, when there fell on his ears what he thought was the name of Madame de Saint Valery. Mr. Inigo was by this time speaking in an important undertone; and Carew, unwilling to play the part of an eavesdropper, opened his eyes, and was about to make himself visible. At this moment, however, one of Mr. Inigo's friends exclaimed with a loud laugh, 'Get away with you, Inigo: you've been after her yourself, you old sinner!' Carew would not for worlds have missed what he then saw. Mr. Inigo

made several playful gestures, indicative of
a juvenile desire to decapitate his friend
with a cane; and then with a delighted
knowingness he leered at him through his
glasses. A second later he started so
that his glasses fell from his nose. He
had suddenly seen Carew. Had Carew been
a ghost, the effect could not have been
greater. Mr. Inigo looked for a moment as
if he would like to make his escape; but,
recovering his self-possession with a super-
human effort, he slowly turned on the ap-
parition the tails of his frock-coat; and
thrusting his hands into his trousers pockets,
he stared at the street from the middle of
a bay-window. Carew's eyelids gradually
dropped again; and he fell into a sleep this
time so sound, that when he awoke from it,
it was his first and most natural impulse to
stare about, and discover what had disturbed
him.

There was a movement and an excitement in the room which there certainly had not been half an hour ago. The number of members had increased, and they were all of them clustering round the two windows, peering into the street, and talking together in tones of expectation. What had happened or was about to happen Carew could not possibly conjecture; but towards one of the windows he presently made his way; and as he did so, he saw that in the middle of the other was standing erect the figure of Mr. Inigo, so perfectly motionless that it might have passed for a portion of the building. A variety of indignant feelings were just beginning to assert themselves, when his ears caught something of what his neighbours were saying, and Mr. Inigo was in a single moment forgotten. 'They're coming this way.' 'They are a worse lot than those of yesterday.' 'The police say they are powerless.' Such were the remarks that his neighbours were interchanging.

'What is it?' he asked, turning to an acquaintance. 'Who's coming? What will be worse than yesterday?' The man addressed stared at him. 'I,' said Carew, 'know nothing. I have but this morning returned to England.'

'Haven't you heard?' said the other. 'It's the mob. They are coming this way.'

'Here they are! here they are!' cried a dozen voices at once; and the group at the window pressed as near to the panes as possible.

'Tell me,' said Carew, still persevering in his inquiries, 'who is it? What is it? For goodness sake tell me.'

'It is the mob—the unemployed,' was the answer. 'They are led by the professional agitators. You'll see for yourself in a minute or two. Listen to that! There they are!'

Carew did listen, and now his ears comprehended a confused and approaching noise of shouts, shrieks, groans, and the trampling of innumerable feet; and in another moment, added to this, came the crashing of broken glass, and outbursts of yelling laughter. At last he got so far into the bay-window as to be able to see down the street; and what met his eyes was a black advancing mass, moving like some great volume of semi-liquid sewage, on the surface of which certain raised objects seemed floating, whilst the edges of it, in one place or another, were perpetually frothing against the sides of the shops and houses. A moment more, and this hoarse and horrible inundation was flowing past the windows at which he himself was standing; and he then began to understand its character better. Considering the stones that were flying in all directions, the position he occupied was no doubt one of danger; but neither he, nor any of the other members, showed any inclination to quit it. The spectacle below seemed somehow to fascinate all of them.

A long procession of discoloured and pitiable faces was slowly defiling by; some looking down with a sullen and dull stolidity, others fixing their eyes with a stare of ferocious wonder at the impassive group watching them : but beyond the shaking of an occasional fist, that blank stare at first was the only sign of animosity. The attention of the mob was concentrated on the opposite side of the street, where a certain University club displayed a frontage composed almost entirely of plate-glass and of window-frames. At the sight of this structure, as if it acted like a signal, a chorus of yells and groans burst suddenly from the multitude, and a storm of missiles began to assail the windows. About this special attack there was a determination and a violence which, so far as Carew could see, had been wanting elsewhere. To smash the glass was not nearly enough ; but showers of stones were poured into the rooms through the apertures, and presently, with a noise that thundered across the street, a heavy chandelier fell crashing from the ceiling of the reading-room.

'That's his club,' exclaimed several of Carew's fellow-spectators. 'It's the club he was kicked out of for advocating the assassination of Ministers.'

'See,' cried another, 'there he is himself—the man in the waggon, with a red flag in his hand.'

Carew could make nothing out of these mysterious observations, but craning his head forward he looked in the direction indicated ; and there was a sight which at once made the matter clear to him. One of those raised objects, which he had already seen from a distance, was now approaching; and it proved to be what his neighbours had just hinted. It was a huge open waggon drawn by four horses. On the shafts, and on the sides, were seated perhaps a dozen men, wildly gesticulating to the crowd. Whatever they were, they were plainly not English workmen. Their long, lank hair, and their wild moustaches, which waved and bristled, with an affectation of ruffianly dandyism, said at least as much as that.

Carew glanced for a moment at this cluster of scarecrows, and then his eyes fixed themselves on a figure which rose above them. This was a man seated in a rude arm-chair, which had been propped up on a packing-case. If his satellites looked wild, he looked a great deal wilder; not, indeed, in respect of his dress or hair, for in that way his appearance was quiet and common enough : but he was shouting to those around him like a maniac loose from Bedlam, and waving the red flag which he held, with corresponding gestures. Sometimes he seemed to use it as a sign of encouragement, sometimes to indicate some particular building. Meanwhile his eyes were starting out of his head; and his whole face was flickering with the livid gleam of insanity. Carew started at the spectacle. This figure was Foreman.

When the waggon reached the club, which was the special object of attack, it halted; the crowd moved round it like water about a rock; and Foreman began to shout with a voice of redoubled emphasis. Most of what he said Carew failed to catch; but several times he distinguished such broken phrases as 'Blood for blood, I tell you,' and 'A life for a life.' Finally this was audible: 'Is there no food in there, think you? Those men know how to get it, and so might you, who deserve it more than they do. What keeps your bellies empty ? Not want of food in the country, but want of courage in yourselves. You're afraid—that's what you are ! But what is it you fear ? Better to die fighting, I tell you, than die starving ! '

The words did not fall idly. The harangue was not ended before a rush was made for the doors of the shattered club. At the threshold there was a fierce but short struggle ; then, whatever opposition there was was overborne, and a crowd of squalid forms swarmed into the interior. Presently, from the broken windows a number of incongruous objects began to be hurled into the street—books, the cushions of sofas, and, in a moment more, cabbages, joints of meat, and various other eatables. All of these the mob pitched wildly about, with shouts of derision, and finally trampled them under foot—all except one leg of mutton, which, having found its way to the opposite side of the street, finished by being pitched against the window next that in which Carew was stationed. This incident, to him only partly visible, elicited a shout of laughter, which, though certainly sufficiently sinister, had more in it of derisive amusement than of mere brute ferocity. It was so loud and sudden that it attracted the attention of Foreman, who, turning round, and having stared for a few moments, began to swell the clamour with hysterical merriment of his own. 'Eggs!' he shouted to the men around him; 'eggs! eggs!' And in another instant, following the course of the mutton, a shower of eggs came hurtling towards the fated window. Oddly enough, something of the laughter of the street seemed to find an echo amongst the members of the club themselves. Carew moved back into the room to see what possibly could have happened; and the first thing that met his eyes was a rapidly retreating object, which looked not unlike a gigantic running daffodil. A second glance revealed to him what this rarity was. It was nothing else than Mr. Inigo, yellow from head to foot with the yolks of a hundred eggs —eggs which, plainly, were exceedingly far from fresh.

'It was done in an instant,' said one of the men who had been near him. 'Foreman —or whatever the devil's name is in the cart there—pointed him out to his myrmidons, who, to say the truth, are d——d good shots with their beastliness. Before Inigo knew where he was he was completely covered in front, and the moment he turned his back, his back was in the same condition. What's become of him now? Gone off, is he, to clean himself? Hang him! I declare that first he ought to have himself photographed. What do you say, Carew? It is a duty he owes to history.'

Another shout from outside recalled both the speakers to the window. The crowd in St. James's Street had by this time almost passed; indeed, little was left of it but a more or less straggling rear. But the dense mass was pouring itself into Piccadilly, and there a scene was beginning of far more savage excitement. Stones were flying with greater force and frequency; the noise of broken glass was more sustained and ominous; and, presently, a member came rushing into the club from Bennet Street, with his hat crushed, and his coat and waistcoat torn, bringing the news that all the shops were being looted. At the same moment another member, who had quitted the room a couple of minutes previously, was heard bringing other news, which received a far louder welcome. 'What do you think, now!' he exclaimed, 'Inigo will die happy. One of the mob has called him a "bl——y aristocrat."'

When some alarming event actually happens before our eyes we often accept it with a dull apathetic coolness, which, when imagining it beforehand, we should hardly conceive possible. This was the case with Carew now. No sooner had the mob quitted St. James's Street than he quietly subsided into the chair in which he had before been dozing, and, picking up the paper which was lately so void of interest to him, he became at once absorbed in it.

There he learnt that during the last two days there had been demonstrations of working men in various parts of London, their object being to call public attention to the extent and depth of the distress then prevalent, and to the number of those who were absolutely without any employment. These demonstrations in the first instance had been orderly, both in their programme and in their conduct. Following close as they did on the

Parliamentary elections, the chief idea in the minds of their original promoters was to impress the new members—the majority of whom were Conservatives—with the gravity of the crisis under which so many of their constituents were suffering. But in each case, or nearly so, these meetings had been broken up, and turned, as far as possible, into a savage and menacing riot by organized gangs under the direction of the League of Social Democrats— a body made desperate by their late defeat at the polls, and anxious to turn to their purpose every form of popular suffering. Carew gathered further that an immense mass meeting had been convened that very day in Trafalgar Square; and at it resolutions of a more or less Conservative character were to have been put to the unemployed by certain of their most competent leaders. He gathered also that in this case, as in the others, the

Social Democrats were known to contemplate interference, and that some disturbance was accordingly thought probable.

This was all he could learn from the morning's paper; but he had hardly done reading it before a succession of telegrams began to arrive, and took up the broken narrative. Everything had happened exactly as had been anticipated, with only two exceptions. The body of men which the Socialist leaders had brought with them was far larger and far more promiscuous; their own disciples were mixed in it with the vilest dregs of the population, and thieves and theorists were shouting side by side; their own speeches, too, had been unprecedented in violence and ferocity, and were evidently designed to promote some actual outbreak. In addition to this, from some unexplained reason, the police, like the witches in Macbeth, seemed to have 'made themselves air,' and there was not a sign to be seen anywhere that law and order had a single official guardian.

Here, indeed, there was matter for grave reflection; and, quite unconscious how time was going, Carew seized on another of the papers, whose columns were full of discussions on the present condition of the labour-market and the sufferings of the labouring classes. At Glasgow, Leicester, Birmingham, Northampton, in nearly every town, the same distress was prevalent. There was the same cry—now fierce, now lamentable—from thousands upon thousands of men, all presumably honest, who asked for no gift of food, but merely for the means of earning it; and how to supply these means, except, perhaps, for the moment, was a question which seemed to astound and baffle everybody. There was a long succession of letters addressed to the Editor about it, but Carew's eyes strayed through a good half-dozen of them without being caught by anything that seemed worth his attention. At least four out of those he looked at were by clergymen, and though not defending any resort to violence, certainly tended to palliate it by the pity they expressed for the sufferers, and the sensational pictures drawn of the popular misery.

On reading these a sense of irritation seized him, and all his own opinions on economic and social subjects, which he had been forming so anxiously and carefully with the help of Mr. Stanley, woke in his mind from the sleep into which Miss Capel had thrown them, as suddenly as the inmates woke in the Palace of the Sleeping Beauty. Jumping up from his chair, he went to one of the writing-tables, and, taking the largest sheet of paper he could find, addressed the following letter himself to the journal he had just been reading.

'SIR,—I am probably quite as humane as

most people, and am quite as much touched by the sorrow and wants of others. But in cases like the present it seems to me wholly wrong to approach the public or the Government through the sense of pity. The ills of the body politic are like those of the individual body. They require in the doctor who is to cure them, not pity, but knowledge and self-possession. Indeed pity, if not kept strictly in order, tends to make the use of knowledge impossible. If a surgeon who is to operate on me begins to cry over his instruments, I shall distrust his skill rather than thank him for his sympathy; and the best security I can have for his doing his best for me will be simply the importance of my cure to himself.

'It is just the same with the statesman when dealing with any popular misery. In his capacity of a statesman, such misery ought to concern him, not on account of what the miserable suffer themselves, but because their misery is a danger to the entire community. An Irish agitator not long since described education as a kind of moral dynamite; and of education as he conceived it—that is to say, as a tissue of ignorant and rancorous lies—the description is no doubt true: but, applied to misery, it is even truer. Its exactness is absolutely perfect. Masses of men who, under existing social conditions, suddenly fall from comparative prosperity into privation, and see before them no hope for the future, become dangerous by the laws of social chemistry, as surely as, under chemical treatment, do the harmless materials of dynamite. Like dynamite, too, they are not self-exploding. They remain dumb and impassive till the fuse is applied by the agitator. Then an explosion follows. It is useless to blame the people. The agitator alone is guilty, and there is no guilt in the world of so deep a dye as his. Could he ensure a new order of things by blowing up the old, we might, perhaps, call him a hero; but the only result of his explosion is, that the people themselves are crushed under whatever ruin they have caused. The structure of society still remains unchanged, or changed only in being for a short time disjointed.

'There remains, however, also this question for society to consider. Is it, in the present and prospective condition of trade, secreting a constant or a growing mass of explosive misery? If so, there is serious trouble ahead for us. It may not be the fault of society, it may be its misfortune only, that this misery is secreted by it; it will not be the fault of the miserable if they cause misery as well as suffer it. Blame is equally useless and equally inapplicable in either case; but unless this diseased secretion can be checked, it is impossible for a sane man to imagine that, in such a country as England, society can ever again experience its old security. Neither poppy nor mandragora will ever medicine it to that sound state which, up till lately, we have been accustomed to consider natural to it.'

Carew, when he had written this, which he did with care, and had re-read it, was conscious, as he said to himself, of feeling somehow a man again. 'Blame the people!' he repeated as he put his letter into the box. 'Poor devils! Why, as I watched the crowd just now, I was far more inclined to cry over the sight than to be angry at it. As for Foreman and his crew, I would willingly string the lot of them up to a lamp-post. But the others—even the roughs and thieves —*sunt lacrymæ rerum.* They are the tears of things, and they are the riddle of things.'

In the middle of these reflections the striking of a clock roused him. He looked at his watch, and found, to his great surprise, that it was high time for him to be hastening back to his chambers. When he emerged from his club the street was perfectly quiet; but, for the first time, he realized the violence of the tempest that had passed. As he crossed Piccadilly there was hardly a house westward which, so far as a glance could inform him, had not suffered damage of some kind. Several jewellers' shops, the windows of which were generally glittering, were nothing now but so many black openings, which scared-looking men were hastily protecting with shutters; and the whole pavement in front of a well-known fruit-dealer's was a singular pulp of trodden flowers and pineapples. In Mayfair, however, everything was just as usual. Cabs and carriages were passing and repassing, just as if no disturbance had happened within a hundred miles; footmen were knocking at doors; ladies were leaving cards ; and Carew found, when he reached his rooms, that his servant had not heard of there being any riot at all. He began to feel as if the whole affair had been a dream ; and thoughts of Miss Capel, the Esterel mountains, howling mobs, broken windows, and, lastly, the kneeling figure of Miss Consuelo Burton at Mass, came floating through his brain in dizzy and quick succession. But on his way to the station he was recalled sharply to the sense that he was moving in a world of realities. He came again across the track of the rioters, who had apparently made their way up South Audley Street and Park Lane also, as in both of these thoroughfares there was hardly a shop or house which had not a window broken or else a door defaced. 'And to think,' he said to himself, when he was at length seated in the train, and was slowly gliding out from under the arches of Paddington, 'to think that it was only two short days ago that a girl's eyes, looking at me in a forest of fairyland, seemed to me to mean either the failure or the success of a lifetime!'

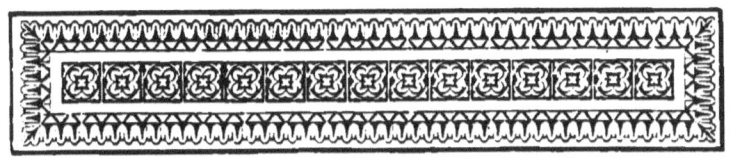

CHAPTER III.

WHEN he reached his own station it was very nearly eleven. The moon was shining brightly, and he received a curious shock as he recognized the outlines of the tall familiar hedgerows, the unmended thatch of a barn on the far side of the road, the line of white palings which fenced in the platform, and the old-fashioned brougham that was awaiting him just beyond them. Stranger still seemed to him the turnings in the narrow lanes that he had known from boyhood, the gates he had swung on under his nurse's tutelage, and the very ditches where once he had stooped for watercress. All was the same, and yet, in a way, how changed! In one miniature creek he recollected he had lost a knife, his treasure when he was seven years old, and he felt half inclined now to jump out of the carriage and look for it. Presently shining like a linen sheet in the dimness, there came in sight the first outlying cottage of Otterton. Carew, in his childhood, had paid many a happy visit there. He could see at this moment the row of mugs on the dresser, and feel again on his tongue the taste of the delicious cider. The face of the old man who lived there seemed again to beam on him, and the wife, half deference and half affection, to drop a delighted curtsey. In his mind's eye he saw them both; but, like the brothers of Helen, 'them the life-giving earth hid now' in the village churchyard. Presently he was entering the village street itself—a long irregular line of silent sleeping dwellings ; and now the carriage had sharply turned a corner, and beyond him lay what looked like a world of shadow and of woodland.

Against this background something was gleaming dimly. It was a lofty arch between two decaying lodges. Carew leaned his head out to take in every detail of this structure. In one window a faint light was glimmering ; over the archway was a huge stone scutcheon, intricate with illegible quarterings ; there was a heavy gate in the very act of being opened ; there was an old woman in a white cap who curtsied ; and in another moment the carriage had passed by her, gravel was crunching under it, and the moonlight was dimmed with trees.

Carew, as he breathed the air, felt it was charged with memories. The very soul of the earth in which his family had been rooted seemed to be floating in the smell of the damp dead leaves. Presently he had quitted the wood and was speeding through the open park, where the moonlight undulated white over far-reaching knolls and glades, and slid in a sluggish film on the waters of a noiseless river. Now there came into view immemorial clumps of elm-trees, and a long avenue meeting the distant sky-line; and a gathering consciousness of what his family was, of what it was to be the heir of so many centuries, came from the shadows and the branches and invaded his imagination. Now he was passing the gabled house of the gardener, now the long walls of the old-fashioned kitchen-garden. Now the carriage had rumbled under the arch of a lofty gate-house; a row of out-buildings capped with a line of turrets was seen for a moment dimly stretching away from him; and at last a plunge through a grove of enormous ilexes brought him out before a vision of old towers and oriels, part of which plainly belonged to an inhabited house, but the more striking of which were just as plainly ruinous.

The butler who opened the door, a tremulous grey-haired man, greeted Carew with so solemn a smile of welcome as to fill him at once with some vague presentiment of evil.

'I'm glad you've come, sir,' he said. 'We've been in a bad way here.' Carew asked him to what it was he alluded. 'It's not the Squire, sir; he's much the same as usual. It's Mr. Horace. Hush, sir, go softly. He's in the west bedroom, and a noise in the hall may wake him. The doctor's been here twice to-day; and he has to-night a nurse who is sitting up with him. There's supper, sir, in the small library, and Mrs. Samuel has got the Countess's room ready for you, because your own, she thought, was too near Mr. Horace's. The doctor says he must have no sound to disturb him.'

Carew, the following morning, was roused from a heavy sleep by his servant undoing the tall creaking shutters; and his eyes were hardly well free from drowsiness before in the man's aspect he detected a certain gravity, which, when he announced the hour, was still more unmistakable.

'It's eight o'clock, sir,' he said. There was a pause. He then continued: 'Have you heard, sir? There's bad news. Mr. Horace, sir, died about four o'clock this morning.'

From the moment Carew had entered the house he had felt in the air a cold presentiment of death; but this had not made him the better able to bear it. It merely increased the solemnity of the event, with the added solemnity of a dim prophecy verified. He asked a few of the ordinary questions as to the manner in which the end had come, and he learned that his uncle had died in a kind of a stupor, itself so like death that the nurse could hardly tell at what moment actual death had happened.

As he descended the broad stairs, with their worn Brussels carpet, he saw that the blinds had already been drawn down. Crossing a long gallery, towards the room in which he was to breakfast, he dropped a book he was carrying on the bare oak floor, and a flock of echoes instantly filled the air, like so many startled pigeons. Picking the book up, he saw the butler standing a little way off, and holding a door open; and he looked at him with an air of apology for the noise that had just been made. The old man understood the look perfectly.

'Ah, sir,' he said, 'you needn't go softly now. Mr. Horace sleeps too sound for any of us to wake him. I was to say, sir,' he added presently, as he was uncovering the dishes on the breakfast-table, 'that the Squire would be glad to see you at half-past twelve.'

Carew had thus the whole morning to himself, and he welcomed that prospect as much as he could welcome anything. Directly his breakfast was over he had an interview with the nurse. He learnt from her every detail she had to tell him, and then, for a few moments, visited the bed of death, and watched the upturned face that lay on the white pillow, as clear and quiet as if moulded in yellow wax. 'Ah,' thought Carew, amongst many other reflections, 'Mr. Inigo will play no more whist with you, or haunt your dinner-table to scrape acquaintance with peers.'

This brief visit over, he wandered out of doors, and avoiding as far as possible every gardener or domestic, he roamed about, contemplating the house and its precincts, and struggling as he did so to collect his disordered thoughts. The house had in former days been the largest in the West of England, and had once consisted of an irregular pile of buildings, towers and cloisters, and long barnlike outhouses, ranged together round an enormous oblong court. But of this one side had little left but the foundations; and two of the others, though still stately, were ruinous. Specially stately in its ruin was a magnificent baronial hall, which Carew's uncle, being too poor to repair it, had been forced to unroof some forty years ago; and now the tracery of its beautiful Gothic windows showed like skeletons with the sky shining through them. One side of the quadrangle only was now inhabited, and even this formed a house of no small dimensions, though one end of it had been cut off from the rest, and had been let to the tenant who rented the home-farm. The slope that rose in the background was shadowy with magnificent timber. Old-fashioned laurel hedges gleamed below; above was the clang of the rooks in the boughs of the leafless elm; and, peering over the sloping slates and the chimneys, the tower of the parish church showed its belfry windows and its battlements.

Carew moved from point to point, absorbing the spectacle, with its many meanings, into himself. Everything he saw was, he felt, a part of him; he, he felt, was himself a part of everything. Not a single object on which he could rest his eyes, even to the pollard on the farthest hill blotted against the sky, was unconnected with his own name and family. They, for eight hundred years, had been the rulers and the centre of all the life around them. They were part of the landscape; they were part of the trees and earth. So far as traditions extended, they had always been kind landlords, and, so long as they could be, generous ones. There was not a house within miles in which their name had not been reverenced as if it were almost royal. Every pinnacle on the house was part of their fossil history. The church walls were hidden with their hatchments and mural tablets. His grandmother's monument almost dwarfed the altar, the chronicle of her virtues being upheld by two cherubs, the one hugging her coat of arms, and the other in triumph, brandishing her crown of glory. 'Nothing,' thought Carew, 'nothing can alter this. We may be swept away, but we can never be replaced. We may have a new race of manufacturing plutocrats, rising and falling like so many golden sandhills. They may eclipse us in splendour, but they never will be what we are. They never will have their roots in the historic life of the country. They will never be, like us, the aristocracy of traditional England.'

The surrounding objects which had suggested these thoughts seemed also to repeat and to draw them out like a fugue. The air was keen with the smell of yet unmelted frost;

and a silvery steam rose slowly from the grass and floated across the gloom of the gnarled and solemn tree-trunks. To Carew these sights and smells were as part of his own mental condition, the mind and the senses interpenetrating and explaining each other.

Presently from the church tower boomed the deep note of a bell. A long pause ensued, and then another followed it. They were tolling for his uncle's death. The sound roused him to a consciousness of his own personal situation. Had the second will of the dead man been signed? With sudden distinctness this question came to him; and yet, though he knew that something important hung upon it, it was some moments before he could recollect what. With an effort he did recollect; and then, like a reflection in some transparent water, which, the moment the eye catches it, obscures the pebbles at the bottom, a vision of blue skies and of palm-trees, and Miss

Capel's face recalling him to the land of roses, floated between his heart and the visible scene before him. All his perplexities were now mapped out distinctly. The possibility of his retaining the family estates, or at all events doing his duty by them, and restoring the family prosperity, depended on his possession of his dead uncle's fortune. Would he find that the dead hand had so ordered his future that the choice lay for him between his family and Miss Capel, and that he must be false to his interest in either one or the other? And if so which choice should he make?

In answering this latter question his imagination wavered; but he found as he examined himself that his will was already fixed. Much as it might cost him to renounce all thoughts of Miss Capel, it hardly seemed to him now within the range of conceivable possibilities that he should with his eyes open renounce his family for her. He looked again at his old ancestral surroundings, at the moss-grown slated roofs, and the ivied walls that were roofless, and he thought, 'You are more to me than any woman's heart in the world.'

Whether or no he would continue to maintain this decision, he had not long to wait before he learnt decisively that he had at any rate not been at superfluous trouble in forming it. At the hour named he was ushered into the Squire's study. It was a room which had been furnished and decorated, during the stately Georgian period, by the same ancestor who had built the house in London; and it was well in keeping with the aspect of its present possessor. The Squire was a perfect type of a race that is now fast dying. The cut of his pale whiskers and the locks of his grey wig connected him visibly with the præ-popular epoch; and the placid smile that dwelt on his lips and eyelids were the smile of a man so accustomed to obedient deference that he could very rarely have had occasion for frowning. Holding out to Carew a delicate wrinkled hand, he expressed quietly his pleasure at seeing him, and then, with an equal quiet, spoke of his brother's death. His manner conveyed no impression of heartlessness—he was not a heartless man; but extreme old age learns to accept everything, and the breaking of no link can much affect those for whom, in a few years at farthest, all links will be broken—broken or reunited. The Squire then proceeded to say that he had telegraphed for the family lawyer, whose presence for several reasons would be desirable; and he handed Carew a paper with a long list of names on it.

'I should be glad,' he said, 'if you will write letters to these, and let them know what has happened—together with the date of the funeral, on which I have already decided. I thought at first of making my servant do so. A business letter he can manage well enough; but the confounded fellow,' said the Squire, still quiet as ever, 'the confounded fellow would bungle over a matter like this. And now,' he went on, when Carew had undertaken the commission, 'there's another little affair about which I wished to speak to you. Your poor Uncle Horace had got some ridiculous notion into his head that you were likely to make a fool of yourself with some French adventuress. He had arranged in his mind the whole course of the drama, though, as he had never seen her, it was clever in him to be able to do so. You were first to disgrace her by making her your mistress, and then to disgrace yourself by making her your wife. Of course the whole thing is a mare's-nest; but, anyhow, he has been at the trouble of making a new will in consequence. Perhaps he has already taken steps to let you know this?' Carew admitted that such was the case. 'I told him,' the Squire continued, 'that it was a monstrous waste of trouble; but last week he had been hearing some nonsense about you in London, and nothing would persuade him that he was not perfectly right. Practically to you it can make no possible difference; and, at all events, now there is no use regretting it. It was only yesterday morning that this new will was signed, and I was one of the witnesses. By the way,' he added as his nephew was leaving the room, 'I had a letter from your sister this morning, with a poor account of your mother. After things here are finished, you'll no doubt go over and see them.'

CHAPTER IV.

AREW'S days between his uncle's death and the funeral were passed in a noiseless and almost monastic seclusion. The lawyer arrived with as little delay as possible—a spectacled freckled old man, who but for his confidential intonation was like a country gentleman far more than a solicitor. Carew was glad of his friendly and sustaining presence, and passed with him nearly the whole of the subsequent mornings, visiting farms and cottages, examining their dilapidated condition, and

learning afresh and in all possible detail the hopeless extent to which the property was encumbered.

'I am as good a Tory,' said the lawyer, wiping his spectacles, 'I am as good a Tory as any man in England, and should as much regret any legislation that tended to break up the estates of the old families. But I am bound to say, Mr. Carew, and I think you will agree with me, that when an estate is in the condition of this one, it becomes an abuse which the law should not perpetuate. Unless its old possessors acquire the means of doing their duty by it the old possessors ought to go. This I believe as firmly as any Radical. I differ from the Radical only in one point. He would cackle over any excuse for their dispossession. I should break my heart over its necessity. However,' he added, 'that case is not yours. It sometimes sounds indecent, when a relation is hardly dead, to begin reckoning up the advantages his death will bring one; but we are speaking now not so much of yourself as of your family; and I am, Mr. Carew, in a position to tell you positively that you are at this moment the possessor of three hundred thousand pounds. Two-thirds of that sum will enable you to pay off every mortgage on this property, which else, sooner or later, I am certain would have to go. Several men have had their eyes on it already; indeed the bailiff tells me that there's a man here now—he's been living in the largest of those two stucco villas—who would buy you out to-morrow had he only the chance of doing so. At least that's the gossip about here. Unless, however,' he added, smiling, ' you forfeit your new inheritance, I trust the Carews may reign here for many a generation yet. Yes—I trust the day by-and-by will come when you may not only be able to restore your own home, but be blessed as a benefactor in every home about you.'

'I agree,' said Carew, sadly, 'I agree thoroughly with the view you take of families in such a position as ours. If we exist only as an abuse we had better not exist at all.'

'You,' replied the other, 'may exist otherwise; though I fear that, as matters have turned out, there will be more difficulty than you perhaps anticipate in applying your fortune to the purposes we have just spoken of.'

Carew inquired to what kind of difficulty he alluded.

'By-and-by,' said the lawyer, 'you will be able to understand it more completely; but I can, in a general way, put the matter intelligibly before you now. Mr. Horace Carew's wish, as you know, was so to leave his money as to deter you from making a certain marriage; and he has compassed that end by placing a deterring penalty on your marriage with anyone not a British subject. Now you will of course see that if, in the event of such a marriage, it was his intention that all his money—for this is your uncle's arrangement—that all his money, except a small portion, should pass from you to a distant relation of his wife's, he could not leave it in your power to employ the principal, at your discretion, in paying off the mortgages on the acres that you are bound to inherit. He wished, indeed, that you should have that power, but he was determined you should not have it until the contingency he dreaded was an impossibility. Accordingly, though, unless you marry an alien, the interest of the money left you will be paid to you during your life, you will not be able to dispose of a single penny of the principal unless and until you marry some born British subject. I can only trust that, vexatious as the condition is, and I am sure quite uncalled for, it will not be found one difficult or distasteful to fulfil.'

This conversation took place the day after the lawyer's arrival; and now the situation, under its most homely and practical aspect, was beginning to stare Carew very full in the face. There were two points in it which he had not before realized, in addition to those relating to his marriage or abstention from marriage. In the first place, he learnt that, as the heir to his elder uncle, he would be a far poorer man than he had had any idea of. In the second place, as the heir to his younger uncle, he would be, in fact he was, a far richer one. The alternatives before him surprised him by the sharpness of their contrast. On the one side was the complete ruin of his family— more complete and more inevitable than despondency had ever foreshadowed to him. On the other was its restoration to power, splendour, and beneficence, greater and more certain than he had ever ventured to hope.

During the whole afternoon of that day and the next he roamed about like a restless ghost, through the glades of the park, through the unweeded walks of the garden, with their furlongs of straggling laurel, through the roofless hall, through ivied vestiges of the cloisters, and again through the corridors of the inhabited house itself, his whole mind in a ferment. Generations of dingy ancestors peered at him from shadowy walls; here and there, distinct amongst the pale tribe, were one or two fine Vandykes; and in a low hall, with a faint smell of wood-smoke in it, there were eight tall Sir Joshuas. One of these, which was hung close to the door, was so placed that whenever the door opened, the key struck the canvas, and had knocked a ragged hole in it: and in this stately and magnificent picture, which, if uncared for, would in a few years be ruined, Carew seemed to recognize an image of his own family. 'Could he,' he asked himself, 'allow all this to go? Did he not owe to it, as it were, a filial duty? Was he not bound to save, and, if possible, to transmit it to a descendant? Could he, for the sake of any private affection, be a traitor to this trust, which, if gone, would be gone for ever?' Everything, from the crumbling towers outside to the rudest oak bench and frayed matting within, from the faintest daub in feminine watercolour fading on the wall in its tarnished frame for a century, to the sixty-four quarterings of his great-great-grandfather, which stained the daylight on the great staircase window—everything he felt to be indescribably a part of himself, bone of his bone, flesh of his flesh. He could not suffer it to be torn away from him.

'Had I a brother,' he said to himself,

'who might take my place—to whom all this money would go, in case I was to forfeit it, I would say to him "Take it." He might take the estates too. But of all our name, there is nobody left but me. I am not myself only; I am a family, I am an institution: and as such, I represent that principle which alone makes, or can make, civilization worth preserving. Anyhow I think so; and if the thought is a folly, I can at least give my folly some dignity by suffering for it.'

The tone of his resolution remained pretty much like this till after his uncle's funeral, when he left Otterton for his mother's. Her home was an old manor house some twenty miles distant—small, but in its own way perfect. A tall rookery rose directly behind it, whose branches overshadowed the white clustering chimneys. A lime-avenue and a garden of stocks and wall-flowers made a world of quiet in front. Inside, there was china and an odour of *pot-pourri*, straight-backed chairs standing on faded Turkey carpets, and rows of calf-bound volumes such as 'Tom Jones,' and 'The Spectator.'

Closely as Otterton was connected with Carew's life, the Manor was connected with it in a yet more intimate way; and just as in his present frame of mind the associations of the one pained and stimulated him, so did those of the other lull, caress, and fawn on him. The waves of thought and feeling were still with him in the state of hush, that they are in so often with those who have come from a house of death; and all the homely and kindly days of his childhood rose up in his memory as he arrived, filling him with a longing for rest, and a wish that he could again subside on them. The old grey-haired man-servant, who welcomed him smiling at the door, with his striped waistcoat, his white silk stockings, and pink cheeks like an apple, seemed to him like one of his own relations; and as he dined with his sister in what was known as the little parlour, the rest he longed for he almost thought he had found.

His mother that evening he was not able to see. She had been for some years failing, and, as Mrs. Harley had told the Miss Burtons, Carew had always shown himself a most good and attentive son to her. But her condition was such that, though always a ground of anxiety, and though one from which she could never recover, it might still be protracted for an indefinite time longer; and except for an occasional sinking, to which her family now were accustomed, she gave no graver cause for solicitude at one time than another. It happened that the present was one of her times of weakness, and instead of dozing as usual, though a calm afternoon, in the drawing-room, for the past few days she had not quitted her bed. She had often, however, been much weaker before, and there was nothing to interfere with the flow of reciprocal information that pleasantly took place between the brother and sister. What had happened to the family in this or in that cottage, whether Mary Ann had married the young man that she used to walk with, and whether the auctioneer's daughter still wore blue gloves on Sundays— on all these little points Carew asked for enlightenment; and especially as to who was the stranger who was living in the larger of the two villas near Otterton. But the last question was one which his sister could not answer.

Late the following morning his mother was in a condition to receive him. She was still in bed, and had just finished her breakfast. Her weakness had long been such that her pleasure at the sight of him had found better expression in her face than in her slow and feeble articulation. It was so this morning as she just turned her head on his entrance. No words could have said to him more than that slight and difficult movement; and he saw looking at him out of those dimmed and well-known eyes all the years of his life, and seventy-eight years of the century. The interview did not last long, nor was there much said at it; but the scene throughout the morning was strongly stamped on his memory. On a table beside the bed were the remains of her small breakfast —a piece of broken toast and an egg-cup with its hollow shell. Beneath her chin, too, there still remained a napkin; and on this a little of the yolk of the egg had fallen. Under ordinary circumstances nothing so offended Carew as the slightest untidiness in anyone's ways at table; but now when he thought of the hands and lips grown helpless that had once for him been the signs of such strength and help, this small and unsightly detail subdued his mind with a feeling which had been quite strange to it hitherto, and he bowed his head in reverence for the sacred weakness of age.

During the rest of the day he poked about with his sister, amongst old chests and cabinets filled with various relics; and they had been half touched and half amused at discovering an entire fossil childhood, in a collection of toys and lesson-books. These had lately been disturbed to make room for some other lumber; and they thought of inquiring of the servants as to the fate of some objects that were missing. This question was, however, in part answered by an accident; for, passing through the diminutive stable-yard, their eyes chanced to be attracted by something red on a rubbish-heap; and going nearer, and using his stick to assist him, Carew recognized amongst dead leaves and cinders, the morocco covers of his diary when he was ten years old, which had then seemed to him a marvel of sumptuous splendour, and which still, no doubt, contained, in the damp and dirt, the tremulous records of his hopeful unclouded life. He looked again, and a worm was crawling over it. 'What fools the servants are!' he exclaimed in a moment's petulance. 'I feel almost as if they had pushed me in there myself.'

These occupations, and the thoughts suggested by them, at first filled his mind completely: but by-and-by, through them and intermixed with them other thoughts came also, gently pushing and asserting themselves. Here was a house, here were surroundings, where a man might live in comfort on no immoderate fortune. If he valued respectable antiquity and family associations, if he valued mellow refinement contrasting with mushroom finery, surely he had that here. Might he not brave the chance of having to let Otterton go, and beg Violet Capel to make a home here with him? Over and over again he asked himself this question, the girl's eyes and lips pleading with him to say 'Yes' to it; and more than once he repeated those lines of Thackeray's which Foreman had quoted in a very different temper—'Love *omnia vincit*, is immeasurably above all ambition, more precious than wealth, more noble than name. He knows not life who knows not that; he hath not felt the highest faculty of the soul who hath not enjoyed it. In the name of my wife I write the completion of hope and the summit of happiness. To have such love is the one blessing in comparison of which all earthly joy is of no value; and to think of her is to praise God.'

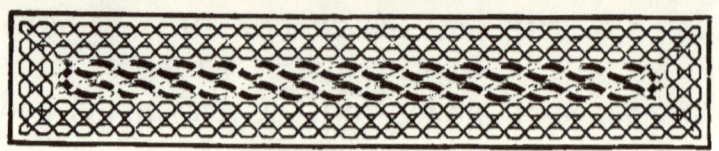

CHAPTER V.

THE following morning Carew was sitting in the library toasting his feet on the brass fender. He was looking at a pile of newspapers that lay on an old spinet; he was reproaching himself for having scarcely so much as opened them, and he was still mainly occupied with thoughts about Miss Capel, when his sister entered, and said in a hurried tone that she thought their mother's state was worse than it had been yesterday. 'In fact——' she added. 'But perhaps you will come upstairs with me.'

They went. His sister entered the room before him. There was perfect silence in it. He at first saw nothing but the bed-curtains. Then he moved softly round to the foot of the bed; and there all revealed itself. Black with her back to the light was the bending figure of the nurse; and carefully propped up on the pillows a still face rested, with that yellow wax-like bloom on it, the meaning of which he already knew so well.

The end had been sudden. His mother evidently had begun her breakfast as usual. It was there on the little table. Slight and trivial things become sometimes full of meaning, and Carew's eye fell on the half-drunk cup of tea and the egg half eaten. He knew at the moment that he should never forget the look of them. The breakfast and those dead lips—ten minutes ago how closely and commonly they were related; and now between them was all the width of eternity—between that smeared egg with the spoon in it, and the life that mysteriously was not.

This event, as was not unnatural, completely changed, for the time, the whole tenour of his thoughts. Miss Capel's image, though he did not intentionally dismiss it, now receded at once out of the ken of his consciousness. The inevitable business matters for the next few days occupied the practical faculties both of himself and his sister; and as for his thoughts, though he affected no conventional gloom, they kept a silent vigil over the strange something that had happened. He recalled what someone had said on the ramparts at Courbon-Loubet—that there are things in life which, however much we may talk of them, are to each, till he feels them himself, as new and as strange as death; and amongst these, he learnt, was the death of one near to him. It was some time, indeed, before his imagination could grasp it; and after having asked his sister some questions she was unable to answer—questions mostly connected with the past and with the neighbourhood, he heard himself saying, 'Well, we will ask my mother.' And then again his mind would imperfectly correct him—'I mean,' he would add, 'when she comes back.'

His feelings, as was natural, were deep rather than poignant. They sank down into his heart rather than wounded or crushed it, and affected his views of life more than his views of his own life. But at the funeral—at this second funeral, so closely following on the other, he felt at least for a moment how sharp a sting death can have for the living.

On his way to the ceremony, which took place at Otterton, reflections such as these kept on recurring to him :—'What is half of life but the memories we share with others?

And before we are thirty a half of this half is gone. Before we are half through life we are knee-deep in the waters of death.' Then by-and-by came the short pilgrimage to the church, and there sounded in his ears the opening words of that office which, whether a man believe or whether he disbelieve, is more moving and terrible than any tragedy ever written, bringing him face to face with all that is worth hoping for, or else with the thought that all hopes are vain. The extreme simplicity, too, of the whole proceedings touched him—the church with its square pews, its huge pulpit and reading-desk, the arms of Carew on every panel of the gallery, the lion and the unicorn keeping guard over the altar, and the absence of anyone except a few neighbours and the villagers.

All those impressions, solemnly as he received them, he could take in and assimilate more or less as a philosopher; but it was different when, leaving the church, they stood by the grave's brink—for it was always his mother's wish to lie, not in the vault, but in the churchyard. He had not realized fully the personal import of it all to him till he saw descending actually into that horrible gash in the earth—that cold insulting mud, that damp and streaming clay—the thing which but yesterday he would have sheltered from the least wind or from a raindrop. He thought of his diary, and how he had seen it on the rubbish-heap; and now, the mother who had given him that diary—they were casting her into a rubbish heap yet more hideous; they were doing to her what he had lately shuddered to see done even to a little morsel of morocco.

He bit his lip. Every nerve was strained to prevent his feelings finding some natural outlet. At last, just before those assembled separated, he raised his eyes, venturing to look about him, and there, standing by the grave on the side opposite to him, was an object that proved a new trial to his fortitude. It was an old woman ten years older than his mother, who had begun life as his mother's maid, and who had never, till her strength failed her, left the service of the family. For many years now she had been settled in a cottage, and Carew was not aware that she was any longer living. She seemed to have risen from the dead to take her last look at the dead.

Presently he went up to her, and taking her by both the hands, 'Nancy,' he said, 'and don't you remember me?' She looked at him doubtfully; he then explained who he was, and a light of recognition like the last ray of a sunset suddenly lit up the old woman's face. She seized his hand again, and began to speak to him of her memories—both of his childhood and his mother's; and then ended, with a glance towards the grave, 'I shall be going to join her there soon. I ought to have gone already.'

'And I too,' said Carew, as he turned away from her. 'We both of us belong to a world that is dead or dying.'

His sister and he were to remain at the Hall for the present; they had neither of them yet decided on their immediate movements in the future—and the rest of the day was passed in the vacant quiet which so often succeeds an event like that of the morning. On Carew's mind there was vaguely an impression as if it was Sunday; his very thoughts seemed afraid to stir themselves into their common secular activity. Next morning, however, an unforeseen incident roused them.

He had wandered away after breakfast into a remoter part of the park, trying to review calmly his situation as regarded Miss Capel. His feelings about her were pretty much what they had been when the shock of his mother's death had rendered them, as it were, insensible; and now slowly and faintly they were coming to life again, untouched as yet by the hostile associations of Otterton. His tenderness for the girl was once more asserting itself; his imagination once more in its mirror was showing him the magic of her eyes. Wholly occupied with these inward events, he passed mechanically through a door in the park wall, and continued his walk in the public road outside. In a few minutes this brought him to one of the gates — a grandiose entrance between two Georgian lodges, with the coats-of-arms crumbling from the friable stone. Within, there stretched away a long avenue of elms, some of whose boughs lay broken and untouched on the ground, whilst grass and weeds were invading the stony roadway.

By this gate Carew was intending to re-enter; but he paused at a little distance, struck by its mournful aspect, whilst the claims of the family honour gave a timid prick to his conscience. He paused and he looked thoughtfully at it. Suddenly his eye was caught by an unusual object—an exceedingly smart-looking brougham, standing some way off in the road. Moved by his curiosity, he slowly strolled by it. There was no one inside, so he was able to examine it carefully. All over it was a gloss of virgin varnish. There was a gloss that was almost equal on the coats of the horses; and though outside there was no device of any kind, inside there was a profusion of ivory fittings, each one of which was, apparently, florid with some large monogram. In contrast to this—' Or could it,' Carew asked, 'be in keeping with it?'—the coachman and footman held themselves rather slouchingly, and seemed to be indulging themselves in less reserved conversation than is perhaps usual amongst gentlemen's servants when on duty.

Having seen what he could, Carew was turning back, when he descried emerging from the one lodge that was inhabited, a man who seemed, from a distance, to be dressed for Piccadilly or Bond Street. The stranger moved a little way into the road, thrust his hands into his pockets, and began staring at the lodges. Carew by this time was within some thirty feet of him; and was so struck by his unexplained presence and his behaviour, that, leaning against a gate, he began to watch him curiously. Who was he? What was he? Was he the undertaker's man? Was he a doctor? Was he the head of some mourning establishment, come at his sister's order? He might be a doctor, perhaps; and yet, Carew argued, few doctors but those of the lowest class could invest the quiet of their dress with such a loud ostentation of quiet. A second glance showed that he could hardly be the undertaker or the mourning-man, for his trousers had a purple stripe on them, and in his little finger there was embedded a diamond ring. At last he turned, and with his head well in the air, and treating Carew to a blank stare in passing, he entered the brougham, which had already advanced to meet him.

Carew fancied he had seen this man's face before; but, think as he would, he could not remember where. He entered the lodge, and inquired of the woman who lived there if she knew the stranger's name, and what it was he wanted. The woman said she had seen him several times lately, walking in the road, and pausing to inspect the lodges; and she gathered—though from what source she did not specify—that he lived somewhere outside the neighbouring town. Then, following what is a common rustic practice, she brought out the only definite part of her answer last.

The stranger, she said, had seen the bailiff talking to her, whom he recognized and at once accosted. He seemed to have something of special importance to say to him, and as it was cold standing in the open air, they had both gone inside and sat by the back-kitchen fire. The bailiff was there now if Mr. Carew wanted to see him, and would no doubt tell him more than she could.

Carew found this to be no more than the truth. The bailiff was full of the interview that had just ended. 'I was wishing, sir,' he said, 'the moment that you came in, to be able to tell you about it before you went away. I did mention, you may remember, at the time of Mr. Horace's funeral, that there was a party residing in the neighbourhood who had his eye upon this property. He's been trying to find out all he can about it; he's been busier than ever since then. Well, sir, that's the gentleman—the gentleman—though to my mind he looks much more like a hair-dresser. He talks to you,' the bailiff continued, in apology for this freedom of speech, 'as if you were no better than the dirt under his feet, and he puts questions to you as if he were hearing you your catechism.'

'Do you know his name?' said Carew.

'I've heard it,' said the bailiff, scratching his head, 'but I don't rightly remember it. I never knew such a gentleman to ask questions. He asks about rents, and leases, and hares and rabbits; and at last he got, sir, to asking about the Squire, and if it wasn't true that the Squire was very hard on the poor. I said, if every rich man had as kind a heart as the Squire—— Snapper, sir—that's his name, sir—it's just come back to me. I thought 'twas a name like one one sees now in the newspapers. Maybe he's some relation.'

'Relation!' exclaimed Carew. 'It's the man himself. The devil's grown a moustache —that was why I did not recognize him.'

He left the lodge in a mood very different from that in which he entered it. Once again his mind was in full activity. It turned from his private emotions to what he conceived to be his duties. 'Let the property pass to a man like that!' he muttered. 'I would sooner never speak to Miss Capel or to any other woman again.'

CHAPTER VI.

AREW'S mind was now fully awake. He suddenly realized in a way which he had not done hitherto the full practical meaning of the large fortune that had been left to him, and the future which that fortune, especially if it became his own absolutely, opened out to him so certainly and so immediately. All his theories as to the duties and the capacities of an aristocracy, all his knowledge and study of the economic problems of the period, he now felt he might begin to translate into definite practice. A sense overcame him of sudden impatient

restlessness. He could no longer live on emotion, or even on thought. His whole moral being craved to be fed with action. His emotion had turned into a hunger for something beyond itself. It no longer sufficed him to reason about the poor and about the people; about the conditions of their employment, the rates of their wages and the cost and quality of their lodging. He longed to feel that there were a certain number of families whose daily lives he could help to order happily; that there was actual distress he might do something to cure; and that he was doing his best to set a real example of that devotion to all whom his power could benefit, which alone, in his estimation, gave power either permanence or dignity.

Under the stirring influences of prospects and thoughts like these, his whole conscience became like a kind of litany—a cry, a supplication to some unnamed Providence, that his life might be granted the development which, and which alone, could complete it.

In most men's lives there have been analogous moments. Their importance is often misunderstood. No doubt, in any such excitement and exaltation of the moral being, in any such passing *clairvoyance* into the conceivable possibilities of life, coupled as it usually is with the desire to make these possibilities facts, judgment, imagination, self-esteem, and hope say a thousand things which are soon seen to be exaggerated, and perhaps may excite a smile. But for all that, they need not be unreal. They are not unreal if, in spite of their apparent exaggeration, they express and for a moment illuminate a tendency which is permanent, but which usually operates in obscurity, and clogged with difficulty and obstruction. Most men would be able to bear witness to this. There are occasional moments, indeed, when the mind is full of oracles, when it hardly knows itself for all the voices filling it. Such moments are the seeds of moral changes, of new departures, though too often they are seeds that never grow.

Of this last fact Carew was perfectly well aware; and several times when, in the course of his meditations, his moral excitement was gaining its completest possession of him, he would sober himself by the prosaic reflection that all the fine things he was saying to himself were addressed to himself as he might be rather than as he was. And then again, as a correction to such moral despondency, he would recall to himself the following pregnant couplet:

> Deeds in hours of insight willed
> May be through hours of gloom fulfilled.[1]

But even now, without waiting for the future, he was aware that these hours of

---

[1] Mr. Matthew Arnold.

insight had had already one practical effect on him. For the first time since he had yielded to the witchery of Miss Capel's presence, he felt that even though he lost her life might be still complete. She was no longer necessary to make his future satisfying. He still knew her charms; he still knew the magic of her wide childlike eyes. She was like sunshine, she was like a perfume, she was like a strain of plaintive music breathing through a garden of roses, or fresh from the breast of a blue southern sea. He knew the power that her nature had over him; but he knew it as he might know the power of a dose of opium, which each time he repeated it would have the same effects, but effects from which, for the time being, he was free. Once more he was master of himself. He felt capable of choosing the life which the thought and experience of years had affirmed and re-affirmed to be the life of rational duty—the only life which could appease his unsatisfied consciousness, and, by affording work to every one of his faculties, would perhaps yield him at last some resting-place for his spirit.

How should he make use of this free interval, in which once more his intellectual conscience was supreme, and passion stood at his feet ready to do its bidding? This was the question he asked himself, and he asked it with a business-like deliberation. 'Any new state of the thoughts, feelings, and desires,' he wrote in his diary as a sort of mental record, 'may be arrested and realized if we can but translate them into action, and this may make a new turning-point for the whole life and character. The danger which I run is that of never translating them into action at all; and if I yield to this danger I know quite well what becomes of me. My life, instead of a structure, is simply a shapeless mound of subsiding aspirations, out of which it is as easy to make any useful career as it would be to mould a statue or a brick out of treacle.'

In this state of critical self-distrust, one image, and only one, came back to him, which brought with it suggestions of action, vigour, and life. This was the image of Miss Consuelo Burton; and even that, for external reasons, was shrouded in a veil of despondency. All the details of their last parting returned to him, and the contemptuous coldness of her last words and her letter. Much, he reflected, might no doubt be explained by some false reports—he did not quite know what—which she had heard of him; and her coldness—this was certainly just possible—might have betrayed interest in him far more than indifference.

'But still,' he asked himself, 'what must be her opinion of me if she is so ready to believe me, at a moment's notice, guilty of anything that could make me deserve such treatment? Probably by this time what interest she may have taken in me has died out, not to be reawakened. Perhaps, after all, there was not much interest ever.' Anyhow, he continued to reflect, it would be very difficult to approach her again, at all events immediately. How to explain matters, or indeed what matters to explain, he did not know. There were no ostensible grounds for any explanation at all. Added to this, he was not certain where she was. Thus, in spite of both the definite conduct and the help and the encouragement to pursue it, which the very thought of her suggested to him, she seemed to his imagination to resemble a light, bright indeed, and sending through the gloom its kindly message of rays to him, but shining in vain over the sheets of a broad intervening water.

His feelings, therefore, will be easily understood—the sudden throb of his heart and the tingling of all his pulses—when he saw one morning, on coming down to breakfast, a re-directed letter for him, bearing a foreign postage-stamp. Was it from Miss Capel ? Was it from Miss Consuelo Burton ? On taking it up he saw that it was from neither; but it did not prove on that account to be any the less interesting.

CHAPTER VII.

AREW'S correspondent was none other than Mrs. Harley. Her letter was dated 'Rome,' and ran as follows:

'DEAR MR. CAREW,—You must not be surprised at getting a long letter from me; for I have many things to ask you, and many things also to tell you. I am going to begin with my asking.

'What have you been doing with yourself all this long time? We had hoped we might have seen you again at Nice, before we left it; and we were much disappointed that you gave no sign of yourself. We are here till after Easter, with some mutual friends of ours; and after Easter, as I think I told you before, we go, for perhaps a week or so, to the Italian lakes. You were good enough to say that you would get us an order to see the beautiful villa and gardens on the Lago Maggiore which belong to your Milanese relations — the "cousin Alfonso" you have sometimes told us about. If this reaches you in time, will you write to me here, or else to the Poste Restante at Baveno. I wish there was a chance of your being at the villa yourself and doing the honours of the place for us. I know you do go there often, and that it is a sort of second Courbon-Loubet for you. I think that that is all I have to ask you—what have you been doing? will you send me the order? will you be there yourself? I will now go on to tell you things.

'Of course you have heard how our friend Foreman has been distinguishing himself.

He now pretends, as you will have seen in the papers—he has also had the face to write to me to the same effect—that he had nothing to do with these riots, and that they were simply the result of accident. He is frightened out of his life at the prospect of being prosecuted by the Government; and a friend tells me, who saw him a few days ago, that his state of nervousness is something really pitiable. George says he is like some man in Rabelais— would it be Panurge ?—who swore, " By the pavilion of Mars, I fear nothing but danger!" I must, however, do our Socialist this justice : if he does fear danger he certainly does not fear exertion ; for, ill as he is, he went suddenly back to London—I wrote to you at the time about it—not very long after he left Courbon-Loubet. We now see the reason why. I've not the remotest doubt in my own mind that the whole thing was hatching for many weeks beforehand. He was brooding over it whilst he was under your roof. In fact, now one comes to think of it, he told us as much there.

'But, my dear Mr. Carew, my real aim in writing to you is not simply to gossip about Foreman and his vagaries. My real aim is to tell you that I think I can clear up a mystery, the results of which you had every right to feel annoyed at. I mean the recall of Miss Consuelo Burton from your delightful and hospitable house. The subject perhaps is one which is a little delicate to touch upon. However, I think we may contrive to get over the difficulty. After all, what is there to be shy about? I am a woman of the world, writing to a man of the world, and our being what we are gives us this advantage at least, that, whilst I hope our feelings have not become blunted, we are able to speak about them with a convenient and comfortable directness.

'Let me begin, then, by reminding you

that I am perfectly well aware of the way in which rumour once connected your name with that of a certain beautiful though not very respectable lady—the Countess de Saint Valery. I think I know the rights and wrongs of the story pretty accurately. You have spoken about it yourself to me. I am aware too— and so must you be, though you can hardly have been told it directly—that the elder Miss Burtons, at one period of their acquaintance with you, fully believed you to have a serious attachment for their sister—and I must remark in a parenthesis that I don't think you could do better—but this belief was quickly and rudely disturbed by the reports which reached them, and to them seemed reliable, that all the while they were wasting their most Catholic encouragement upon you, and preparing to welcome you into the bosom both of the Church and their family, you were carrying on an intrigue with the person I just mentioned, and that you would have gone off with her yourself if a rival had not forestalled you.

'Well, of course I think myself they were a couple of fools to believe this; but, given the belief, you can hardly wonder at the consequences of it—that they acted as they did, and gave you the cold shoulder. Afterwards, however, they heard another side of the question, and began to suspect that their thoughts about you—which, to do them justice, they never made public—might possibly have been far too severe. Of course that you should know such a person as Madame de Saint Valery at all was an offence in their eyes, and took some of the bloom off your sanctity. Still, you were not hopelessly lost to their favour, and you had a chance of salvation left you in their uncovenanted mercies. When they met you at Nice I was able to be your advocate, and I told them what geese they had been to swallow all that gossip against you; but your best advocate was yourself. The best proof of the good impressions you made is the fact of their allowing me to bring Consuelo with me to stay with you. Of course the presence of Lady Chislehurst and Mr. Stanley had a good deal to do with that; but the impression made on them by you yourself personally had, I am sure, even more; and, as you see, they were becoming quite willing to receive you back again on the old footing.

'Now comes a mystery on which I can throw no light. Perhaps you can. In some way or other you must have offended Mr. Inigo. How, I cannot imagine; but he evidently must have some grudge against you; for what do you think he has been doing? I will tell you.

' Whilst we were staying with you in the château, Elfrida and Mildred were away on some little expedition of their own—I think it was to a convent; and they only returned

on the morning before I and Consuelo left.
They had hardly been in Nice for a couple of
hours when Mr. Inigo found them out and
pounced on them, filling their ears with a
long tale of your iniquities. That Foreman
was staying with you he learnt from Lady
Mangotsfield, for whom, I am told, he had
been constantly on the look-out ever since
Lord Stonehouse introduced him to her. So
this piece of news at once went to Elfrida,
and along with it another, which no doubt
will astonish you. Mr. Inigo asserted that
the reason for your being in the neighbourhood was nothing else but the presence there
of Madame de Saint Valery ; and he added, to
clench matters, that he had himself seen you
leaving her house at twelve o'clock that very
night on which you dined with me. Nor
was this all, but he raked up again all the
old gossip about you, assuring Elfrida that it
was true. How he got her—her and Mildred

too—to listen to him, is more than I am able to say. But it turns out that they did so. Poor things! In intentions, no doubt, they are as harmless as doves; but that kind of harmlessness, when lacking the serpent's wisdom, is very often as bad as the serpent's malice.

'Fancy! this is what they wrote to Consuelo about you—at last I have seen the letter. "We are surprised to hear that Mr. Foreman is staying at the château. We consider it very undesirable"—and so on, and so on; you can imagine the sort of thing. "We also hear that Mr. Carew is engaged to a lady of such a character as to show us that we were mistaken in thinking his house would be a proper place for you to visit at, and we are sure that Lady Chislehurst must be mistaken equally. Anyhow, we must request that you come away at once, and we are writing to Mrs. Harley—though we have told her nothing more than is necessary—to ask her to make your departure as easy and as comfortable as she can for you."

'There! what do you think of that? Perhaps your eyes are opened a little now.

'Luckily, however, there is more to add. There has at last appeared on the scene—I don't know if I remember rightly the little Latin I once on a time learnt—a *deus ex machinâ*, in the person of your old friend and defender Lord Stonehouse. He is not here now, but he has been at Rome for a few days with us; and it was only the day before yesterday that, quite by accident, he found out there had been any trouble about you. I must describe the scene to you. I can't help laughing when I think of it.

'I and the three Burtons were sitting together in the morning, trying to settle what should be our plans for the day, when Lord Stonehouse came in and began talking of some palace he had been visiting.

Amongst other things he said: "There were enough of coats-of-arms there to satisfy even our friend Carew. By the way, Elfrida, where is he? He's such a devoted admirer of yours, you ought to know. You should have brought him to Rome and made him kiss the toe of his Holiness."

'You should have seen the look Elfrida gave him. One could almost have fancied that her face was turned into ice, she seemed so completely to refrigerate the whole room; and as for Consuelo, I only gave one glance at her, and her cheeks were scarlet. Lord Stonehouse, with his curious and almost old-womanish shrewdness, at once saw something was wrong, and looked at Elfrida, smiling out of his screwed-up eyes with a patient patronizing curiosity. Consuelo the next moment went out of the room, and then in an instant, before Elfrida could speak, "My dear Elfrida," he began, "how have I put my foot into it? I am immensely anxious to know!" Nothing would put him off. Elfrida was no match for him; and though she was very unwilling to discuss the subject at all, he soon managed to worm out of her all the stories she had heard about you, and from whom she had heard them. All this she told him with a painful and embarrassed solemnity, as though she were touching pitch and were almost afraid of being defiled by it. And then when all was out, Lord Stonehouse leant forward in his chair, gave a slap to one of his fat knees, and burst into a chuckle of laughter. "That is too rich!" he exclaimed. " Upon my word, that is too rich!"

'Elfrida, at this, was perfectly dumb with astonishment and anger, and put on what Lord Stonehouse calls her "excommunicating face."

'" My dear Elfrida," he said, " do tell me why you are looking so glum. You don't mean to say that you believe this cock-and-bull story, do you?"

'Elfrida told him stiffly that she had only too good grounds for believing it.

'"What grounds?" said Lord Stonehouse. "The chattering of this fellow Inigo? If I hadn't thought you could have taken his measure better I declare I would never have introduced him to you. He's nothing more than a pedlar of second-hand scandal and gossip, which he picks up and alters, and hopes will pass for new; and then when he gets anyone to stop and examine his wares— though no one does so except for the purpose of laughing at them—he imagines that he is mixing in society. Pooh! All this about Carew—I can tell you exactly what the real facts are. Madame de Saint Valery has never seen him but once since he has been here, and that happened quite by accident. He was smoking his cigarette on the Promenade des Anglais, and she happened to be leaning over the balustrade of her garden. I have not the

honour of knowing the good lady herself; but
a Russian acquaintance of mine, Prince Olgorouki, whose shoes our friend Inigo was under
a kind of contract to lick, knows her exceedingly well; and I heard of it all from him.
He himself had heard it from Madame de Saint
Valery; and she, I believe, had spoken of it
to him because she wanted to know where
Carew was living, and was very much ag-
grieved at his not having been to call on her."

'At this moment Lady Chislehurst entered
the room, and hearing your name mentioned,
insisted on learning what was being said about
you. She knew that something had gone
wrong, but was not quite sure what; except
that there had been an unpleasantness in connection with Foreman's visit, and now for
the first time she was told the whole truth of
the matter. At once a discussion began about
your intimacy with the lady in London, and
your whole former acquaintance with her;

and Lady Chislehurst at once took up the cudgels for you—with excellent effect. She, as you know, has a wonderful knowledge of gossip; in fact, with regard to anyone who is suspected of Catholic leanings, she is a kind of epitomized Inquisition—I am bound to say, a most kind and charitable one. Though she is determined to know the worst, she always hopes for the best; and she was able to tell Elfrida, with every air of authority, that the worst about you in this connection was certainly not very bad.

'As for Consuelo, I don't know that I have anything special to add. I think it will be enough for you to be simply told that she too knows what her sisters know. She knows you have been judged wrongly.

'Out of that intelligence I must leave you to make what you can or what you choose; and I will only add that when next you meet the Burton family, if they are at first a little

shy of you—I don't know that they will be :
I only say if they are—the only reason will
be, not that they think you deserve ill of
them, but that they feel they have acted
unfairly and perhaps foolishly by you.

'And now I am going to return to the
subject of our own plans. In about ten days'
time we leave Rome, as I have already told
you, for the Italian lakes ; and I will at last
reveal to you that the mutual friends who
are going with us are none other than the
three Burtons, together with Lady Chislehurst and Mr. Stanley. It is just possible,
too, that Lord Aiden may join us there, after
he has paid a solitary visit to the Lake of
Garda, and enjoyed on the peninsula of
Catullus the tunes that his own mind will
play to him. We shall probably ourselves
make a number of expeditions, but our head-
quarters will be Baveno, just opposite your
cousin's island villa. Don't let me put you

to any trouble; but if without trouble you can do so, you will, I am sure, send us an order for seeing it. I only wish there was any chance of your coming that way yourself. Happy man, with all these foreign relations! Even Foreman will not be able to deprive you of every place of refuge at once.'

Carew felt, on laying down this letter, as if a sudden break had come in a sky of grey clouds, and a sun, whose existence had almost become incredible, were beginning to brighten through them. At once a change came over his whole mind. His power of resolution again began to assert itself; and his plans for the future, up till now so undecided, with a strange rapidity assumed a practical shape.

His altered condition might have been detected in his step when he rose from breakfast. He moved towards the library like a man with a definite purpose, and wrote letter after letter with an air of business-like rapidity. He then inquired for his sister, who had not been yet downstairs, and had presently a conversation with her as to her movements in the immediate future. What she told him he found perfectly satisfactory; and his next step was to request an interview with the Squire. This was graciously granted; and before the hour of luncheon it was known to the whole household that owing to some sudden news Carew would be leaving Otterton by dawn the following morning.

BOOK V.

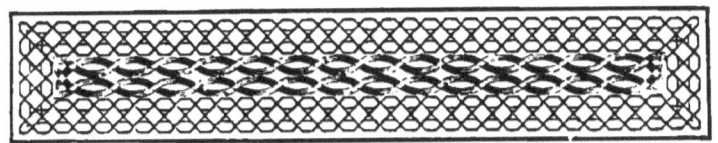

CHAPTER I.

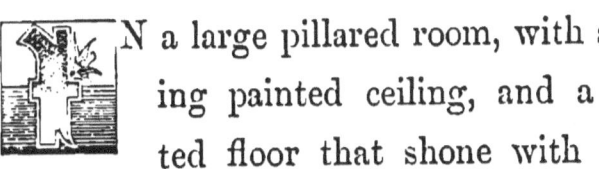N a large pillared room, with an echoing painted ceiling, and a tesselated floor that shone with reflected statuary, a man was seated alone at a small table in the centre, having just finished his solitary evening meal. A pile of fruit which glowed and gleamed in the candle-light was lying untasted before him; and sometimes his gaze would rest listlessly upon this, sometimes it would wander round the florid unhomely walls, whose friezes and medallions were now almost lost in shadow.

Presently rousing himself, he tinkled a

silver hand-bell, and, whilst awaiting the coffee for which this was the signal, produced from his pocket a letter in a clear female hand, and, spreading it open before him, began to read, or rather to contemplate it. An expression of pained perplexity gathered on his face as he did so; and at last, with a deep sigh, he abruptly rose from his seat and opened one of the windows.

Outside, a night palpitating with starlight and dewy with scents of flowers, revealed a balustraded terrace and tall classical vases. Beyond these, from a garden that lay below, masses of dark foliage just raised themselves into sight; and again beyond these, between the tops of cypresses and oleander-blossoms, was the moonlight faint upon a lake that floated under a boundary of mountains.

The man, bare-headed, stepped out upon

the terrace, and inhaled the air as if it gave him a kind of comfort. Then he moved to a spot at a short distance from the window, and fixed his eyes on the lights of some small town, that was visible from thence on the far side of the water, glimmering at the foot of the mountains like the sparks of a fallen rocket.

'By this time,' he exclaimed to himself, 'they must be there, all of them—there amongst those lights. And I—how shall I meet them? To-morrow I shall be coming to the turning-point of my life—to the day, or the few days that will give their character to years. How much, at times, hangs on the choice of a moment! How much, at times, on our making no choice at all! We say to ourselves with regard to some course of action, "We will think about it and call again," as if we were speaking to a shopman; and when we do call again, the thing we might have chosen is gone. Never, never, never can we recall the wasted opportunity. We forget that life is a journey which can only be travelled once. There are no circular tours in it.'

The letter which he had been looking at indoors he still held in his hand, and he now crushed it with a sudden and painful contraction of his fingers; then for a moment he raised it and sorrowfully pressed it to his lips. A minute or two later, he started as if he had come to a resolution. Returning to the dining-room, he again rang the bell, and, scribbling hastily a short note in pencil, confided it to a servant, with some brief directions and inquiries. Once more he sought his former station on the terrace; and folding his arms, he remained there staring motionless at the lake.

This man was Carew.

Five minutes elapsed, and not a sound

broke the stillness; then there rose from below the whisper of dipping oars, and presently a boat, or rather a dim blot on the waters, was seen moving straight towards the cluster of lights opposite. An hour or so later it again became visible returning, and Carew was still on the terrace, at once watchful and preoccupied. He waited there till he heard footsteps approaching, and directly after a letter was brought out to him — a letter which at once he hastened indoors to read.

'My dear Carew,' it ran, 'you tell me that you are in some great perplexity. You want my advice, and you want it, you say, instantly—before the beginning of the probable meetings of to-morrow. As to those meetings you are certainly quite right, for by to-morrow afternoon the whole party will have assembled here—Lady Chislehurst, the three Miss Burtons, the Harleys, and Lord Aiden. The Harleys, indeed, are here already, and Mrs. Harley has duly informed the others that you hope to see and welcome them as soon as possible after their arrival. If, therefore, you wish to consult me about anything, I will be with you at breakfast —let us say at about nine o'clock. I think, a little later, you may expect Mrs. Harley, who has just had some singular news which she wishes herself to communicate to you.

'So many of your perplexities have, I know, been cleared up, that I am a little at a loss to conjecture why you write so dejectedly. However, I can imagine that there may be a point or two as to which you may think me able to make you feel more at ease ; and any hint or information which I may be able to give you, I shall give with the greatest pleasure, and hope it may prove useful to you. No doubt at present I am writing a little in the dark. Until the very day before I started from Rome, I had not a notion that

you were not still at Courbon-Loubet, and now
I find that you have been for weeks in England, and that you have suffered a loss for
which, my dear Carew, you will know I feel
deeper sympathy than can be expressed in
a note like this.

'Ever yours,

'Frederic Stanley.'

The following morning, by the time
named in the letter, Carew was standing at
the landing-place watching for his friend's
arrival. Before him a flight of crescent-shaped granite stairs dipped into the rippling
water. Over him was a canopy of budding
bankshia roses, and a marble satyr behind
him glimmered through the leaves upon its
pedestal. High in the background rose a
series of artificial terraces, supported on walls
and arches which were half-hidden by foliage
—laurels, camellias, myrtles, oleanders, and
cypresses. Here and there through valleys of

flowers and verdure there were glimpses of urns and statues, and small fantastic temples, or the spray of a fountain floating like a tissue of white crape; and crowning all were the parapets and topmost windows of a palazzo.

Such was the place to which, acting on Mrs. Harley's suggestion, Carew had betaken himself directly after receiving her letter. Everything thus far had fallen out as he had hoped it would—everything at least which, at that juncture, he had reckoned upon. And yet his brow was clouded; it betrayed neither hope nor resolution; his air was as listless and anxious as it had been a week back at Otterton. The morning was bright everywhere except upon his face. Something or other he plainly had on his mind, and it was this which he was now waiting to unburden to Mr. Stanley.

Confession, whatever relief it may bring

eventually, is rarely at the time a very delightful process, and Carew, when he saw Mr. Stanley's boat approaching, had an uneasy feeling as if he were about to submit himself to his dentist. Mr. Stanley's very first words, however, at once made him feel more comfortable. There was about them, as about his manner usually, a certain pleasant, half-humorous matter-of-factness which, when he was discussing any grave or delicate subject, put any awkwardness or false shame out of the question. No one, in fact, could approach a case of sentimental casuistry with more sympathy and with less sentimentality than he.

It was an inexpressible relief to Carew to see on the priest's brow no annoying reflection of the cloud that obscured his own. It was an inexpressible relief to hear him, the moment he was landed, instead of attuning his voice to a note of anxious solicitude, declare that he was dying of hunger and could talk about nothing till he had breakfasted; and then, as they went up to the house, falsify this statement by launching into exclamations of delight at the fairyland of gardens that burst upon him. They were presently seated at breakfast in a small carpetless room, that was gaily frescoed with shepherds, temples, and goddesses; and a voluble parrot in a glittering gilded cage was making them smile with unexpected scraps of Italian. All these surroundings formed natural subject for conversation, and rapidly paved the way, without any effort or awkwardness, for that other subject which Carew was anxious to touch upon.

'No,' said Mr. Stanley, 'I was never here before; nor, till a very few days ago, had I any notion that you were here. I thought, as I told you in my note, that you still were at Courbon-Loubet.'

'And I,' said Carew, 'till I got Mrs.

Harley's letter, was equally ignorant as to the movements of all of my guests at the château —all except Foreman : I learnt quite enough about him.'

'I think,' said Mr. Stanley, smiling, 'you will learn something more to-day.'

'About Foreman?' exclaimed Carew. 'What on earth have I to learn about Foreman? And why do you laugh when you speak about him? One would think there was some mystery.'

'Well,' said Mr. Stanley, 'if there is one, Mrs. Harley will reveal it to you. She has made me promise to leave that pleasure to her.'

'You know, I suppose,' said Carew, 'that she has revealed one mystery to me already? You know that she wrote to me, don't you? and what the things were that she explained to me?'

'Perfectly,' said Mr. Stanley, 'perfectly ;

and I was delighted to hear she had done so. Of course you refer to the mischief that was made by that good gentleman Inigo; and I can well understand—or at least, my dear Carew, I think I can—all the annoyances which must have been suffered both by yourself and Miss Consuelo Burton.'

'It was about that,' said Carew, 'that I wished to speak to you. When one meets one's friends again after a certain rupture it is sometimes a little difficult to know exactly how one stands with them; and a good deal depends on one's understanding one's position accurately.'

'Well,' said Mr. Stanley, 'with regard to the elder sisters, your position is just what it was when you last met them at Nice—or rather, you are higher in their favour. You must surely realize that, by their eagerness to come and visit you here. Your perplexity, surely, cannot refer to them.'

'Not altogether,' said Carew, 'and yet partly. I am thinking how best to explain it.'

'Let me,' said Mr. Stanley, 'hazard the beginning of the explanation, and my guess, if wrong, will at any rate have been complimentary to yourself. You have had, if I am not mistaken, the fortunate penetration to discover the depth of character—one might almost call it the moral genius—of their younger sister; and you wish to know, after what has lately happened, in what frame of mind she is likely to meet you to-morrow. Is not that your meaning?'

'More or less it is,' said Carew, doubtfully.

'Then, in that case,' said Mr. Stanley, 'I need only say about her the same thing that I said about her two elder sisters. She too will meet you as she met you last before there had arisen any of this foolish misunderstanding. I'm afraid, however, that I am talking wide of the mark. Judging by your face, we are not on the right subject yet.'

'We are not,' said Carew, with some slight hesitation. 'I am glad to hear what you tell me; but it was not what I was most perplexed about. I didn't so much want to ask you anything about her feelings towards me, but as to her impression, and the impression formed by her sisters, as to my feelings towards her. I merely speak to you, my dear Stanley, as if you were a common observer: I do not want you to betray any confidences, in case her sisters should have spoken about the matter to you. Do you think that she—that Miss Consuelo Burton entertains the idea that I am—well—in any way seriously attracted by her?'

Mr. Stanley stared at Carew in astonishment. 'Do you mean to say,' he exclaimed, 'that you can possibly doubt that?'

'Once,' said Carew, 'I certainly did not

doubt it. I mean in London. I felt sure then that she realized how I appreciated her. I thought, too, that she was growing to appreciate me. But,' he continued wearily, ' times change, people drift apart ; and it often seems to me almost as visionary to hope that such feelings in another would still remain and wait for one, as to hope to find to-morrow some cloud of yesterday's sunset.'

'My good friend,' said Mr. Stanley, 'we are not talking at present about what the young lady feels for you, but about her natural conclusion as to your feelings for her. Let us leave London alone ; let us merely go back to Courbon-Loubet. I don't know— so far as words go—how much or how little you may have said to her. I am referring merely to your whole manner and conduct there. If you did not yourself know what such conduct would seem to mean, one might almost imagine that you did not mean much by it. That, however, I don't believe for a moment; for were that true, one could hardly imagine a case of more bare-faced and more-deliberate trifling.'

'You are right,' said Carew, 'in believing me not to have been trifling. The long and the short, then, of the matter is this: I produced the impression both on her and on others that I wished to marry her, and this wish they will still attribute to me. Is not that what you mean?'

'Certainly,' said Mr. Stanley, 'and it had never occurred to me that you could be in doubt about it.'

'About what, then,' said Carew, 'did you think I wished to speak to you?'

'To tell you the truth,' said Mr. Stanley, 'I was a little puzzled to conjecture. I concluded, however, that, considering the complications which have occurred, you wished to know in what temper she would meet you.

Her manner towards you was much less unequivocal than yours was towards her. I can easily conceive your being in some sort of perplexity, and what I gathered from your note was this—that you thought I might tell you something of how the land lay, and so spare you a little unnecessary embarrassment. Indeed if that was your meaning you were right. I certainly could, without violating any confidence, tell you certain things, which I think it would be well for you to know.'

As Mr. Stanley spoke Carew's eyes brightened. 'Tell me,' he said. 'Tell me whatever you can tell. Yes, it is this—what you speak of—it is this that I wished to consult you about. But what I had wished also, and what I had wished in the first place, to have explained to you, was very much what you have already taken for granted.'

'Explain it to me again,' said Mr. Stanley, 'and explain it in your own way.

If one is to give advice, one can never learn the circumstances too exactly.'

'Well,' said Carew, with an effort assuming a certain dryness of manner, 'there is no need to indulge in the language of sentiment. It will be enough to state my case as if I were writing a Parliamentary Blue-Book. I have come, then, to this conclusion with regard to my own life: I shall be more likely to make a good use of it—indeed, I shall be likely to do so only—if I can find a wife who understands my views and aspirations, who would help and encourage me in putting them into practice, and would redeem them from becoming what I fear they are now—so many useless sighs and so much waste of brain-tissue. So far as my acquaintance extends—and amongst women this is pretty extensive—there is only one person who possesses, or even suggests, the necessary qualifications, and that person is Miss Consuelo Burton; and so important to myself do I consider the settlement of the matter, that I have come to this place for the express purpose of meeting her under favourable circumstances, and arriving at an understanding with her, either one way or the other. So far as she knows, my being here at the same time as herself and her party is nothing more than an accident. Mrs. Harley alone knows otherwise. I don't suppose, though you and she have discussed my affairs together, that she has told even you the real reason of my coming here—that I am here simply in consequence of the information she sent me.'

'No,' said Mr. Stanley. 'She has kept your secret perfectly. All these people conclude that you are here in the natural course of things, taking the lakes as a resting-place on your journey home. They have none of them, to my knowledge, even heard that you have been in England, though the deep mourning in which I grieve to see you will soon oblige them to know the fact. Of course,' he added, 'you got a letter from Miss Elfrida Burton? She wrote to you before leaving Rome.'

'I did,' said Carew, 'and a very kind, frank letter it was. So far as mere ease and pleasantness goes, this evening's meeting will be easy and pleasant enough. What I wanted to ask you as plainly as I decently could I have already asked you: I mean, whether I were distinctly looked upon as anxious to marry Miss Consuelo. That question you have answered. You have also told me that you could tell me something as to what my prospects in that direction were. You said as much as that, didn't you?'

'We have finished breakfast,' said Mr. Stanley. 'Would you mind our coming into the garden? What I have to tell you I can tell you as we are strolling about.'

They did as Mr. Stanley suggested, and for some minutes they both found a relief in suspending their personal conversation and indulging themselves in the enjoyment of the morning.

By-and-by Mr. Stanley began again. 'I cannot,' he said, 'give you a very definite answer with regard to the point you spoke of; not because I am bound to keep secret any special fact that I know, but simply because I have no certain knowledge. If you want a definite answer, you must get that from herself. Still, as I said just now, I have one or two things to tell you which may possibly help to guide you. In the first place, I am glad you have given me this opportunity of expressing the admiration I feel for this girl's singular character, which is still more singular when considered in its relation to your own. What your interests are, my dear Carew—at least, your higher interests—nobody knows better than I. I think, too, that you are perfectly right in your distrust of your own practical resolution. But your instinctive sympathies, and the instinctive bent of your intellect, constantly connect you, as if by a kind of fate, with the special social problems of the present and the near future. In this way she is almost your exact counterpart.'

'You think that?' said Carew. 'That is your real opinion?'

'It is,' said Mr. Stanley. 'I don't want to indulge in any exaggeration, though this beautiful garden is suggestive of poetry; I would much rather imitate you and talk like a Blue-Book; but I must say that Miss Consuelo Burton in many respects reminds me of Saint Theresa. It is the same kind of nature; but, so far as I am able to tell, it is quite without the true monastic vocation. However, I can't speak for certain, and there will lie your difficulty.'

'What!' said Carew. 'Does she think of entering a convent?'

'I believe,' said Mr. Stanley, 'that her thoughts are tending in that direction, though they would certainly not lead her to take the veil at once.' He paused, and a moment later resumed. 'What is special about her, to my mind, is this. Other women, in numbers, have devoted themselves to the service of the poor; but she not only shares the impulse which produces this immemorial devotion: she has realized, in the keenest and most practical way imaginable, the special conditions which distinguish our own epoch, and which present an old duty under a new form. It is not often that the keenness and coolness of masculine logic are united to the passionate sympathy of feminine intuition;

but they are in her. To you a marriage with her would be of incalculable benefit. I am speaking quite calmly, not as the confidant of a lover, but as a kind of moral politician.'

'What,' said Carew, laughing, 'is the good of telling me that, when in the same breath you tell me that, at present, her dearest hope is to renounce marriage with anyone?'

'She is not decided,' said Mr. Stanley. 'Perhaps you might help to decide her. I must tell you, too, that the ideas she connects with a cloister are very different from those of an ordinary would-be nun. Quite apart from any personal interest in her, you will find much in them that is suggestive, and well worthy of thought—especially as they are largely due to her visit to you at Courbon-Loubet.'

'You speak in riddles,' said Carew.

'They are riddles,' said Mr. Stanley, 'which she will be able to answer; and Lady Chislehurst, you may be sure, will insist on her doing so. She is longing that the matter should be fully explained to you.'

'What!' said Carew. 'This is a very odd state of affairs. A girl's private reasons for wishing to enter a cloister are not usually the subject of her general conversation with her friends.'

'You don't understand,' said Mr. Stanley, 'but a couple of days will make you, and perhaps this evening will. Anyhow, Lady Chislehurst won't let the subject sleep. You recollect Miss Consuelo's eagerness—don't you?—when she was staying at the château, about Foreman's Socialistic theories. She at once realized that, alone of all reformers, the Socialists had gone straight to the root of the social difficulty. She also realized that, having once got at the root, there their wisdom ended, and they utterly failed to see what this root was made of.'

'Or rather,' said Carew, 'it was you who

pointed that out to her. The root, you said—with a most happy illustration—was simply human nature. You said that the same causes would prevent our turning a country into a Socialistic commonwealth that would prevent our turning it into a Trappist monastery.'

'Yes,' said Mr. Stanley, 'but I used the illustration without realizing at the moment how accurate and apposite it was. Miss Consuelo Burton understood it instantly, and read a meaning into it beyond what I had put there. She saw——'

'Saw what?' said Carew. 'What is it you are looking at?'

'Look,' said Mr. Stanley, 'who's that in the boat below us? It surely is Mrs. Harley.'

'It is,' said Carew, ' and she is waving her parasol at us. We must go down and meet her.'

'And now,' said Mr. Stanley, 'be prepared for a piece of news. What I began to tell you will keep.'

CHAPTER II.

CAREW'S face during the whole of the late conversation, though sometimes it had lit up with interest, had never lost its fixed air of anxiety, nor, if he had meant to unburden himself of some secret trouble, did he exhibit thus far the least sign that he had done so. The moment, however, he met Mrs. Harley and gave her a hand to help her from the boat to the landing-steps, his eyes brightened and his lips wore a happier smile. Nor, indeed, was this unnatural. Mrs. Harley's face, always brilliant with quick thought and expression, was now prophetic of something so eminently delightful that a sense of expectant humour must have been awakened in all who looked at her.

When the first greetings were over and they were proceeding up to the house, 'I have come,' she said, 'with a piece of special news for you, and I only hope it has not reached you before me.'

Carew said it had not.

'Because,' Mrs. Harley continued, 'it is here—in these newspapers,' and she tapped with a rough brown glove a copy of the *Morning Post* that was blushing under her red umbrella. 'Let us sit down somewhere, and then you shall hear the secret.'

Carew led the way to a huge shady portico that just eluded the dazzling glare of the sunlight, and as soon as they had seated themselves Mrs. Harley unfolded her papers. Whilst she was looking for the passages she wanted the others kept perfect silence.

'Listen,' at last she said, 'listen to this letter. It is addressed to the Editor of the *Morning Post*, and is dated from a club which you, Mr. Carew, belong to, in St. James's Street.

'"SIR,—As an eye-witness of the recent disgraceful riots, I must beg your permission to say a few words. Letters have appeared in all the most influential journals urging that the Government should at once prosecute the ringleaders, in especial the notorious Foreman. At the same time, it has been represented in other quarters that such a prosecution would be futile and unadvisable, either because Foreman and his associates were not really to blame, or else because it would be impossible to bring their guilt home to them. Whether these latter suggestions emanate from those who fear or from those who sympathize with the miscreants, I do not pretend to decide; but I ask you to give publicity to the following facts. I and five or six other gentlemen of the most distinguished social position are prepared to offer evidence so explicit and circumstantial that, were none else forthcoming, it alone would be sufficient to convict Foreman of everything he has popularly been charged with. The riot was practically his creation. It is said to have been planned by him. As to that I naturally know nothing, not being in the habit of associating with agitators and revolutionists. But I do know that it was deliberately led and deliberately directed by him. One event—in itself sufficiently uninteresting—has become known to the public: that he was turned out of a certain University Club which he belonged to owing to his having publicly advocated the murder of a Cabinet Minister; and this club is opposite that from which I am writing. As the rioters were advancing up St. James's Street Foreman ordered a halt directly in front of these windows. I watched the event myself, and heard every word he uttered. I saw him point to the club from which he had himself been ejected, and with violent gesticulations, and expressions of the wildest hatred, urged the attack on it which almost immediately followed. We, who are connected with no political party, and whose only sin is the name of being dandies and fashionable exclusives, were meanwhile allowed the benefit of our obscurity. By accident, however, Foreman caught sight of a group of us, whom it is not impossible he knew well by appearance, as three of us were personages of the very highest rank and distinction; and at once, with an almost maniacal fury, he began to direct the attention of his followers to us, signalling out my unworthy self in particular, and calling for eggs and other disgusting missiles. We had done nothing to irritate the mob—nothing even to attract their attention. If we had not been signalled out by the knowledge and malice of this one man as representatives of the aristocratic classes, we should not have been so much as noticed. I may also add that the attention and ferocity of the mob could not possibly have been directed towards us so rapidly had Foreman not had about him a large and trained contingent from his League of Social Democrats, which embraces, in all probability, some of the most notorious thieves in London. Only let the Government have courage to bring this miscreant to his trial, and I can promise for myself and for my friends that the case for the Crown shall not fail for lack of conclusive and circumstantial evidence. I have the honour to remain, sir, your obedient servant, ——." Then,' said Mrs. Harley, ' follows his name, and after that comes a postscript :

'" P.S.—It only remains for me to add

that I shall be much astonished if this infamous League be not pronounced to be an illegal society; and also, that the man Foreman, if he be not found to merit penal servitude, will only escape that, from being found more fit for an asylum. Little as one is in the way of hearing anything about the private lives of such people, reports are afloat that he is well known by his friends to be subject in private matters to the most extraordinary hallucinations."

'Now who should you think,' said Mrs. Harley, 'is the author of that letter? It is none other than our good friend Mr. Inigo —" Your obedient servant, Geoffry Inigo."'

'I knew it!' said Carew with a laugh of real amusement; and then as the laugh died his look of sadness returned to him.

'Wait a bit,' said Mrs. Harley. 'That is not all. We have not yet come to the part that concerns yourself.'

'Concerns me!' said Carew. 'What has all this to do with me?'

'Listen,' said Mrs. Harley, 'and you will very soon see. I have read you one letter; I will now read you another.'

Carew looked, and saw that she now had in her hand a second newspaper, of a different appearance from the first, which he recognized in another moment as the organ of sensational Radicalism.

'This,' said Mrs. Harley, 'is addressed to the *Pall Mall Gazette*. Listen to it.'

'"Sir,—A letter has appeared lately in the columns of the *Morning Post*, from a certain Mr. Geoffry Inigo, containing a series of false and libellous statements respecting my conduct during the recent regrettable disturbances. I wrote a letter in reply to it to the same journal, which the Editor—with what fairness I leave you to judge—has flatly declined to publish. I must beg you, sir, therefore, as a matter of common justice, to give publicity to the following plain statements, for the truth of which I am not only prepared to vouch, but absolute proofs of which I am enclosing herewith to you.

'" The value of Mr. Inigo's testimony in general may be estimated by what I have to say about it with regard to the two following points.

'" In the first place, he gives us to understand that he is a representative of the aristocracy and the world of fashion. As to the world of fashion I will not presume to speak. It is impossible to say what may not fitly represent *it*. But as to his claims to aristocracy, beyond the fact that he was standing with some Lords and Honourables in a window, his only claims are these. His father was a grocer, in a small way of business in Shrewsbury, and his mother had been cook-housekeeper to a rich attorney in the neighbourhood. Her maiden name was Jane Jennings, and she died in the August of 1868.

'" In the second place, he calls the League of Social Democrats an infamous society, and declares that the law could not hesitate to pronounce it illegal. It may surprise the public to learn—but it is nevertheless quite true—that this same Mr. Inigo has been for the past ten years the largest and most constant of our contributors to the funds of that very society. If he is inclined to deny this, copies of his cheques can be produced in evidence.

'" I can easily imagine that as to this point at least your readers may incline to be sceptical. But the following facts will make what I have said intelligible.

'" This so-called Mr. Inigo is not Mr. Inigo at all. Inigo is, indeed, one of his Christian names, but his real surname is Foreman. He is, in fact, my own half-brother —the child of my father by his first wife.

'" The one thing he dreaded most in the world was any exposure of his parentage; and having quarrelled with me for my indifference to fashionable ambition, he subsequently began to expect that I should claim him as a relative, and so bring disgrace upon him. This idea was entirely his own. It had never entered into my head. But some ten years ago he came to me of his own accord, and told me that, my opinions being so and so, and my conduct being so and so, it would be a serious disadvantage to him were his relationship to me known; and he asked me on what terms I would consent to keep it secret. I at once saw my way to a good thing, and told him that I would hold my peace on condition of his subscribing two hundred pounds annually to the League of Social Democrats. His subscription, which till now has been paid punctually, was due this day a week ago—the day after the riots

—riots which I regret as much as any man, and in which he himself was a slight and accidental sufferer. But no subscription was forthcoming. I wrote to him, and reminded him of the matter, at the same time assuring him that the ill-usage he had received was not designed for a moment to do him serious injury, and expressed neither hatred nor anger on the part of the mob, but simply a supreme and almost good-humoured contempt. Still I received no answer; but instead of an answer to myself, I saw in the *Morning Post* the libellous letter which has prompted me now to address you, hoping that the public will gather from our only circumstantial accuser what is really the trustworthiness of the accusation.

' " I am, sir, yours faithfully,

' " JOSIAH FOREMAN.

' " Office of the League of Social Democrats, Palace Chambers, Westminster."

'There!' exclaimed Mrs. Harley, 'and what do you think of that? Do you see now how the correspondence affects you? Mr. Inigo imagined that you had somehow divined his secret, and was terribly afraid that you would whisper it to some of your friends. Do you recollect the night at Nice when he came in after dinner, and you by accident mentioned Foreman's name to him? Did you see the look he gave you, and the odd change that came over his manner? At the time we none of us could make out what it meant.'

'Yes,' said Carew, 'I recollect it well. God bless my soul! this is really too ridiculous. Don't speak to me for a moment. Let me lean back quietly and be amused at it. My dear Mrs. Harley,' he went on presently, 'it's worth while to have suffered a little annoyance merely to have arrived at so delightful an explanation of it. Of course —of course, everything fits in like the parts of a child's puzzle. If Inigo suspected what you say he suspected at Nice, Foreman's presence at Courbon-Loubet must, of course, have confirmed his suspicions.'

'Of course,' said Mrs. Harley; 'I know it all for a fact. I've just had a letter from Foreman's wife, who tells me about it. Poor woman—for her I am really sorry. She fully believes that her husband will really be imprisoned, and she knows—for it is quite true about his having a touch of madness—that if he only is sentenced to solitary confinement, he will, as Mr. Inigo insinuates, have to march out of his cell into a madhouse. Foreman himself, too, is in a state of most abject terror, as you can see by that letter, which he would never have written if in his senses—terror for his own safety, and rage against Mr. Inigo. Mr. Inigo is the one person for whom I have no manner of pity. Of course it's all very well for us to laugh now; but a man with that spiteful tongue might easily do permanent mischief—and it's no thanks to him that in this case that he hasn't.'

These last words produced a curious change on Carew. The laughter and animation which he had till now exhibited suddenly left his face, and his former look of dejection came over it like nightfall.

At length rousing himself, he said in a mechanical way, 'And where are Lady Chislehurst and the others? Have they arrived yet at Baveno?'

'Lady Chislehurst,' said Mrs. Harley, 'arrived just before I was starting—and with her a Catholic bishop and two atheistic professors—one of them no less a person than the great Mr. Humbert Spender. The Burtons are due at two in the afternoon, and Lord Aiden an hour or two later. I hope you fully realize that you have asked us all to dinner to-night, and Lady Chislehurst begs me to tell you to remember that this will constitute a second meeting of your Society.'

'My dear Carew,' Mr. Stanley here interposed, 'do you know how time has been passing? I must be going back to Baveno.'

Carew turned to him with a look of blank disappointment, and begged him to stay longer. Mr. Stanley, however, said this was impossible; and Mrs. Harley, who declared herself to be equally pressed for time, said she would return in the same boat with Mr. Stanley.

'Well,' said Carew, 'come as early as you can this evening, that we may walk about and look at the place before dinner. Stanley,' he added in a low tone to the priest, 'you have not finished what you began to tell me.'

'Never mind,' said Mr. Stanley, 'you will hear all about it to-night, or some time to-morrow at the farthest.'

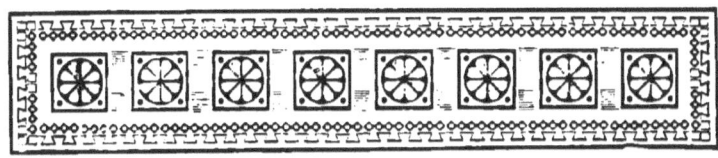

CHAPTER III.

CAREW passed the rest of the day miserably, in dull dejection varied by feverish excitement, till late in the afternoon, when his guests duly made their appearance—the three Burtons, the Harleys, Mr. Stanley, Lord Aiden, and Lady Chislehurst. The meeting was to Carew a surprise from its unmixed pleasantness. Lady Chislehurst was more benignant than ever; and as to the elder Miss Burtons, their frank and half-childish laughter as he came forward to meet them put him at his ease in a way which he had never ventured to hope for.

Not only did they make him feel no new embarrassment, but he found that the little thunderstorm which had now so happily spent itself, had cleared the air of anything that had formerly marred their intercourse.

Nor did Miss Consuelo make matters much more difficult for him. There was a little tremor in her manner and a little blush when he first met her at the landing-place and helped her out of the boat; but whether or no she was really fit for a convent, she had at any rate so much of the knowledge and graceful dignity of the world, that if she felt any awkwardness she was perfectly able to hide it, and to do what so often only women of the world can do—give her eyes and manner the easy frankness of her feelings.

The evening was clear and balmy; the spirit of spring breathed everywhere, and so long as the daylight lasted, melting by luminous stages into transparent dimness, they wandered about the garden, and through the great rooms of the palazzo, examining and discussing whatever happened to strike them, out-of-doors or within, from the landscape to pictures and furniture, and promising themselves a clearer view of all the beauties and curiosities to-morrow.

Just before dinner Mr. Stanley said to Carew, 'Don't try this evening to turn the conversation to that particular topic which we left unfinished this morning. Miss Consuelo Burton would be only annoyed by your doing so. If she has a fault, it is too keen a sense of the ridiculous ; and she said to me, only the last time I talked to her, that she dreaded nothing more than appearing like a woman with a hobby—a female bagman who travelled with one idea—an intellectual monkey who performed one particular trick. To-morrow night, no doubt, we shall hear something of her—well, of her scheme, her plan, her notion—whatever we like to call it; indeed, you may trust Lady Chislehurst for having it well ventilated. But to-night let us be less ambitious. Let the conversation take its course.'

Carew yielded to this advice with the relief often experienced in putting off what is serious ; and he did this with all the more readiness on hearing Lady Chislehurst, true to the character given of her, declare that next day must be a regular *réunion* of their Society, and that, fresh from Rome as they were, there would be no lack of things to talk about. 'I wish,' she added, 'the Bishop would be one of us: and Professor Spender, who is, I believe, the most famous of living scientific philosophers — if we made him an honorary member for an evening, who knows that it might not prove to be a means of grace to him ?'

This latter suggestion was not taken up

by anybody, and the conversation presently lapsed into a pleasant and careless babble, consisting mainly of an interchange of news and impressions from Rome, from London, and Lake Garda, with occasional allusions to the late riots at home, and the ominous destitution that was spreading amongst the industrial classes. To-night, however, these last were allusions only, and were little more than the shadow of the skeleton at a feast, which was animated mainly by a spirit of expectation and rest.

When the diners had sat down there had still been colour in the west—a luminous liquid saffron; but when they rose the face of nature was changed. The stars were out, and the moon was about to rise. Something was said by one of the company about returning, and Carew was addressed on the subject of boats and boatmen. He, however, refused to listen to this.

'It is quite early yet,' he said. 'You can be in no hurry to get back; and if you won't feel cold—and you won't, for the night is as warm as summer—I propose to take you for a little row on the lake. I've arranged everything, and I'm quite sure you will be enchanted.'

The proposal was so pleasant that he had no need to press it; and all the party being well provided with wraps, and the boat being commodious and comfortable, and well-manned with rowers, they felt, as they glided out into the soft gloom, in no hurry to bring the expedition to an end. Presently something occurred which made this opinion grow on them. They had not gone more than a few hundred yards from the island when they saw another boat coming slowly towards them, like an object moving in a dream. Suddenly there arose from it a tinkling sound of music—of a guitar or mandolin struck by a practised hand; then there joined in some other stringed instruments, performing a kind of prelude; and at last came the melody of a rich Italian voice, singing a song half reckless and half tender, the burden of which, at the end of every verse, was taken up by other voices in chorus. All the party exclaimed with delight at this gliding and mysterious orchestra, which now suffered them to approach near to it, and would then elude them and float away into the distance, leaving its music like a vanishing wake behind it. Carew was beset with inquiries as to who the performers could be; and at first replied, laughing, that the lake was 'full of noises,' like Prospero's Island. But he at last admitted that he had planned the entertainment himself, and that the performers were a small troupe—two of them Neapolitans— who happened then to be in the neighbourhood. The music passed from one tune to another with a fairy-like succession of changes, seeming, as if by some magic, to be luring on the boat that followed it; and it kept ahead of them all the way, till the clocks on shore were heard striking eleven, and the party found themselves making for the lights of Baveno.

All were loud in their thanks to Carew, and were regretting that the expedition was so very nearly over, when a cry of 'Listen!' from one or two of them, again called attention to the music. Carew, in particular, became suddenly silent, as if the sound had mesmerized him.

'That song!' exclaimed Lady Chislehurst. 'How well I know it! It is a hymn the Neapolitan fishermen sing to Our Lady in the evening.'

Carew had recognized this fact already. It was the first song he had heard Miss Capel sing.

The whole evening, till this last moment, had been of unexpected, of almost bewildering, pleasure to him. He had neither had, nor tried to have, any intimate conversation with Miss Consuelo Burton. He had been content to give these hours to the natural healing of their friendship, leaving what was more than friendship to assert itself during the days that would follow. But he had been meanwhile observing, with admiring and minute observation, her graces of manner and movement, and even the little niceties of her dress, and the arrangement of her hair. He had been observing this, and connecting it mentally with his knowledge of what solemn and serious things those eyes could look upon which flashed so brightly under that dainty fringe of hair, and how all the gravest hopes and sorrows of life had agitated the breast which was hidden by that pretty Parisian jacket.

But now this song, floating mysteriously across the water, suddenly stirred thoughts alike in his heart and conscience which for some time had been lying soundless and tranquil, and made them move and murmur as a wind makes fallen leaves. He said goodnight to his friends sadly and absently; he arranged for their return to the island next day as if he hardly knew what words he was uttering, and when he was rowed back alone in the now silent boat he had the air of a man who had lost rather than found a treasure.

'Coward that I was!' he exclaimed. 'Stanley might have helped and advised me; but I could not find courage to tell him the only thing which in any serious way made any advice necessary!'

CHAPTER IV.

THE following morning he awoke with a dull sense of apprehension; and as soon as he had time to recollect the cause of it he discovered it to be this. He wished to have the whole of the day till the evening absolutely alone; he feared to be broken in upon by an early arrival of his friends, and he could not remember in the least at what hour he had said he would expect them.

Springing out of bed, he wrote a letter to Mrs. Harley, and despatched it at once by boat, to say that important business had unexpectedly called him away, and that he would not be back to receive them till close upon five o'clock.

'Yes,' he murmured to himself as he sealed the envelope, 'it *is* important, and it was utterly unexpected!'

The day was not far advanced before, acting under an impulse very similar to that which at Courbon-Loubet had driven him on his pilgrimage to St. Paul du Var, he was gliding slowly towards a distant quarter of the lake, under the congenial conduct of a dumb Italian boatman.

A jutting ridge of mountains shut him presently out of sight of Baveno, and as soon as the glitter of the last white house was invisible, with the air of a man who at length finds himself in private, he drew from his pocket a crumpled sheet of paper. It was the letter which two nights ago he had been pondering over during his solitary dinner.

Again he re-read it, lingering over every word. It ran thus :

'I wonder if you will think it wrong of me to write to you as I am going to write. I wonder if you will think it immodest, unwomanly. Some people like women better for being like that; I don't know if you do. I don't know what you will think of me. I might almost say that I do not care; for when a person is in a position like mine, after all, what does anything matter? Do you see what I have come to? Do you see what you have brought me to?

'But it is not you only; and oh! I do not mean to reproach you. It is nothing new that you have done that fills me with this mad longing to write to you. No; it is something else. It is this—how shall I put it?

'It is coming upon me—you know what I mean—sooner than I expected. This suddenness is terrible; and till it came so near I don't think I could have realized—indeed I am sure I did not—what it would be like.

'*He* comes to-morrow; and in ten days we are to be married. To-morrow!—and after that all my life will be behind me.

'I cannot, I will not—no, at least I will stop at that—I will not write to you one word when he is here. It is treachery, of course, to do so now, but it would be doubly treacherous to do so then, when, the moment after I had sent away all my thoughts to you, I should be obliged to pretend that they were still in my eyes for him. A woman may become bad; but that kind of constant deceit and falsehood—never!—oh, not that!

'Perhaps it will bore you, hearing me tell you what I feel for you. Men do get bored if a woman once admits she is fond of them. But never mind; I am a long way off, and you can tear my letter up as soon as you have had enough of it. But you ought to forgive me, for it is yourself whom you have to thank for this—for all this I am inflicting on you. You taught me to do what I am doing now. Do you remember those verses you sent me, in which you said you

> Would never wholly leave me, till betwixt
> My life and yours there is the great gulf fixt?

And till then I don't mean to do so. But, do not be frightened when I say I will not leave you till then; for that "*then*" is to-morrow.

'Oh, once more—since it will be once more only—let me feel that my arms are about your neck—that I am holding you—that I know that you are there, and that I am telling you in your own ear, hiding my eyes against you as I do so, how everything in me fit to be called love has been yours, and is yours still, and how, when it may not belong to you any longer, it will never belong to anyone.

'I don't believe that you understand this at all—no, no, not one small bit. How should you? This is the sort of thing that a man never understands. It is simply the old story. You will go away, and forget, and find someone else. Your having known me will not alter your life in any way; but mine will never—no, never—be the same again. You have shown me what happiness might be; you have taught me to know the taste of it; and, as I cannot ever have that happiness for my own, I shall never now be content with what once perhaps might have contented me. That is all. As I tell you, it is a very simple story; and I don't complain.

'Complain! I should think not. Oh, my—I don't care to call you what I should like to call you—do not be angry with me for writing to you like this, for it was you who made me love you; and do not pity me too much. I do not mean to give way and be dismal. I suppose even, though I say that I shall never be happy again, that in the years to come I shall try to clutch at happiness, or what at the moment seems like it; and perhaps one day I may succeed in forgetting you by making myself no longer fit to remember you. But if I do that, I would sooner you never heard of my having done so, and that you never thought about me again.

'Good-bye! good-bye!—how much that word means now!—and believe that though I shall never be yours at all, the one wish of my heart is that it had been possible for me to be
'Yours always,
'VIOLET.'

To this was added a postscript on another piece of paper, dated the following day:

'I had meant to have told you not to send me any answer. But you may now. I have heard from him again this morning. It is put off for another three whole weeks. He is kept in Paris by business. A line from you, if you will write to me, will be the one good thing this reprieve can bring me. Except for that, it will be merely a prolongation of intense suspense and suffering.'

Carew had arrived at the island, now a few days back, full of hope and confidence. His future at last seemed to be shaping itself in a way that promised to satisfy every need and aspiration that had ever made him respect himself. But he had not been there for four-and-twenty hours before this letter had reached him, having dogged his path from England. The moment he read it it filled him with a disquiet and perplexity for which when at Otterton he had never bargained. Its chief effect was to stimulate not so much his affection as his conscience. His relations with Miss Capel were placed in a new light by it. He had always believed she was in some measure attracted by him; but his belief in this attraction, or rather the extent to which he realized it, obeyed a law which is very far from being singular. He understood her heart entirely by the light of his own. It was only the glow of his own feeling that rendered the signs of her feeling visible to him; and in proportion as his feelings grew sober about her, hers about him—her feelings and her whole position—gradually passed away out of the grasp of his imagination. The result with him was a mental state much more common than many people would like to acknowledge, in which the only moral problem the disposal of his affections presented to him was what would harmonize best with the needs of his own best nature, not what he owed to the needs which he possibly might have awakened in hers.

Accordingly, when he found, as he had found, that another and not Miss Capel was the woman fittest to complete and redeem his life, the one difficulty which he realized as obstructing his path was simply what lingering tenderness Miss Capel might still excite in himself. She was not a claimant to be met, but a temptress to be set aside.

Thus the above letter came like a moral shock to him, and his conscience suddenly roused itself into a state of abnormal activity, which might perhaps seem even greater than such a stimulus could explain, unless account is taken of his state of mind at the time. The letter reached him just at the very crisis when, full of serious, high, and determined thoughts, he was preparing to offer himself to Miss Consuelo Burton. To him, in such an offering, there was something almost sacramental—over and above what constitutes the ordinary sacramentality of marriage. He would, if he married her, be not only offering his faithful companionship to a sympathetic woman : he would be offering her life and his to some great Cause as well. Here was a sacrament and a sacrifice the very desire for which sprang direct out of the highest needs of his nature ; and the mere act of contemplating it made his conscience sensitive—sensitive to an almost morbid degree. For this reason Miss Capel's letter touched him with a keenness that might have been wanting otherwise : and he sorrowfully seemed to himself like a double traitor—a traitor to her, and Miss Consuelo Burton also. If he offered himself to the latter, he would have to confess to her that his heart since their parting had been possessed by another image. That indeed might be forgiven him, and the offer of his heart be accepted, could his confession end there. But he would have to confess also —for he felt now that candour was the one virtue open to him—he would have to confess also that in seeking Miss Consuelo Burton he was seeking his own salvation at the price of another's ruin. He would have to confess to her that, if he knelt with her at the altar, hoping that, with her to guide him, he might find heaven and happiness, the thought of another bride would necessarily come across him, to whom, partly through his conduct, the altar would mean nothing but despair.

Such were the thoughts, such were the feelings, which he had made up his mind to confide to Mr. Stanley, and which, when the time came, he had found himself unable even to touch upon. Mrs. Harley's news about Mr. Inigo, and the subsequent arrival of his other friends, had for the time distracted him, and allowed him to forget his troubles; but the song so unexpectedly sung by his own musicians on the lake, had not only reawakened the voice of his importunate conscience; it had once again vivified his own longing for Miss Capel. This longing, it is true, was more under control than formerly, and it did not efface for a moment the image of Miss Consuelo Burton. But it filled his being with painful and humiliating discord. It came back to him like a distant smell of fir-woods; it came back to him like a voice from a lost Paradise; and though he felt he should be able to master it if necessary, he fully realized that it would cost him some effort to do so.

Such had been his condition last night; such was his condition now as he lay under the awnings at the stern of his lazily-moving boat, which his dumb boatman was directing on a course he had already indicated.

All of a sudden he raised himself from a reclining position, and, sitting up, looked round him. He was not more than a hundred yards from shore, and was slowly rounding a headland covered with luxuriant gardens. The gardens feathered down close to the water's edge, their dense foliage sprinkled with white laurel-blossom and buoyant flower-tufts of the lilac trees. Here and there peeped out an angle of some glimmering villa, and the waves below were gleaming along a succession of granite landing-steps. Presently one villa of more pretension than the others became visible, showing to the lake the whole of its unveiled façade. A trim parterre was in front of it, ornamented with statues and cool with a splashing fountain. Gay blinds sheltered the open windows; and at some of these could be seen the flicker of a transparent curtain. The whole place had somehow an air about it of wealth and refinement, and struck the imagination as a bower of luxurious quiet.

Carew fixed his eyes on it, lost in a reverie. He then wrote in Italian, on the back of an envelope, the following question, which he handed to his mute attendant:

'Who lives now in the villa which was occupied two years ago by the Comtesse de Saint Valery?'

The man, who was well accustomed to this means of communication, replied that he did not know, as the present occupant had arrived but a few days ago; and he added a sentence, whose meaning he emphasized by a gesture, to the effect that they now were at the precise place where the Comtesse had once saved the life of a drowning child.

To Carew this was no news. His mind had gone back to the well-remembered scene already — to his first meeting with that beautiful and unfortunate woman, half shallow in her nature and half noble, made now reckless and now selfish by passion. He seemed to see her again as clearly as though she were really present, dripping with water as he drew her into his own boat, and turning to him a face which now had a new meaning for him : for in that remembered face he now saw an image of Miss Capel, with all the charm in it of which Miss Capel could never divest herself, and all the daring frailty which Miss Capel might ever develop. Little had he thought then how the acquaintance he was making would prove one day the source of the worst of his life's troubles. Silently, moodily, yet with a touch of embittered pleasure, he brooded over the past, which the place and the scene recalled to him ; and when he roused himself and signed that he wished to be returning to the Island, the hard facts of the present seemed harder and more miserable than ever. His friends whom he was about to welcome he would be welcoming under false pretences. Taken as a group, they represented to his imagination a paradise which he was about to enter, but to enter as an alien only, and in which he never could have either part or lot.

CHAPTER V.

AREW'S friends were at the Island before him, so he had no time on arriving for making a moral toilette, but was obliged as best he could to pull himself together at the moment. Lady Chislehurst did much to make this operation easy, for the simple reason that she instantly made it necessary. She was full of news of the most various and interesting kinds. She had been sitting half the afternoon with her bishop and her two atheistic philosophers; and she had herself been tendering much practical instruction to the former, and hear-

ing him in turn make argumentative mincemeat of the latter. In addition to this, the newspapers of the day were full of alarming accounts from the United States and from Belgium. The late riots in London had acted as a signal to the revolutionary labour party all over the world. On the great American railways the traffic had been totally suspended; in Belgian towns and villages factories had been burnt to ashes. Strikes, with a threatening of armed rebellion in the background, seemed to be everywhere spreading themselves with the rapidity of some terrible conflagration.

His thoughts being hurried away by these practical matters, Carew was able for the time to forget his private perplexities, and he entered into the conversation with as much interest as usual, till at last these impersonal subjects took gradually a personal colouring.

'I can't say,' murmured Lord Aiden

at dinner, 'that I myself am at all a prey to panic.'

'But at any rate,' Mrs. Harley retorted, 'you must be a prey to pity. These strikers and rioters may very likely be mad, but it is a kind of madness that is mainly produced by misery.'

'No doubt,' said Lord Aiden, 'the present is a period of distress. These economic diseases of the modern world are very much what the plague was to the Middle Ages, and are as little to be cured by revolution or agitation.'

'No,' said Mrs. Harley, 'but their recurrence may perhaps be prevented—just, Lord Aiden, as that of the plague has been—by some gradual change in the social condition of the people.'

'I doubt,' said Mr. Stanley, sadly, 'if it is good to be too sanguine. It is true, as you say, that the plague has ceased to visit us; we have also protected ourselves more or less against the ravages of smallpox. But are we protected against disease in general? Do we see our way to dispensing with either doctors or hospitals? To me, I must say, it seems utterly visionary to expect a time when economic distress shall be impossible ; and the true point to which we should direct our endeavours is the care and relief of sufferers rather than the extinction of suffering. The highest thing for the practical man to aim at is the best that is practicable, not the best that is imaginable. For the politician, as the politician, there are no counsels of perfection.'

'Precisely,' exclaimed Lady Chislehurst. 'Now there's a bit of wisdom—I wish, Mrs. Harley, you would realize this fact—which is Catholic all over. The Catholic Church indulges in no illusions. It produces saints, but it knows that its chief work is with sinners, and will be so till the end of the world comes.'

'And we think,' said Mrs. Harley, 'I think, and Consuelo thinks—that the way to get at the sinners is to get at the outer circumstances that make half of the world's sins inevitable. Consuelo, may I tell Lady Chislehurst what you said to me this morning? I am sure you have the courage of your opinions.'

The two elder Miss Burtons looked towards their sister with an odd mixture of affectionate wonder and anxiety as she quietly said, 'You may.'

'Well,' said Lady Chislehurst, gracious but inquisitorial, 'what was it?'

'It was this,' said Mrs. Harley—'I don't know whether it will shock you. She said that a home which a decent man can respect has as much to do with holiness as have all the Seven Sacraments.'

The elder Miss Burtons certainly did look shocked, but as for Lady Chislehurst, to Mrs.

Harley's surprise, she showed no sign of displeasure except a momentary twitch of her eyebrows, and replied, in a voice that had all her usual sweetness, 'Had Consuelo said that some three or four weeks ago, and before I knew, as I do now, what it is she is thinking of, I should be sorry to hear that she had let herself use such language. Even now I think that the language itself is wrong, but as to her meaning it will do all of us good to think of it. Come, Mr. Carew, I have something particular to say to you. Have you forgotten that we here are not merely a dinner-party, but that we are members of a certain Society? There are some things which perhaps we can talk of better when we are out of the noise of knives and forks and wine-glasses; but if, by-and-by, we may sit in the western portico and watch the remains of the sunset, which I am quite sure must be lovely, I shall insist on our taking up the discussion which we left unfinished on the terrace at Courbon-Loubet.'

'By all means,' said Carew; 'I could wish for nothing better.'

'Do you remember,' said Lady Chislehurst, 'how you showed us your room, your books, and your labours on Political Economy? You contributed some ideas to us there. We have brought some from Rome which we are going to offer to you; yes, and to you too, Mr. and Mrs. Harley, for I think you have heard but little of these yet.'

With regard to the sunset Lady Chislehurst was perfectly right; and though the stars were sparkling when the party settled themselves in the portico, the heart of the west was still alive with rose-colour.

'Well,' exclaimed Harley, whilst the servants were going round with coffee and Lord Aiden was lighting a cigarette, his constant comforter, 'no doubt for us it is a very delightful thing to look across lakes and gardens at purple mountains and sunsets, and talk about the sorrows of men who live in back-yards and alleys. It is delightful to dream of the new duty which we owe them, and new ways of discharging it. It's a delightful intellectual exercise, just as Plato's "Republic" was. But after all, do we, any of us, really think that we shall ever be led to any new discovery? As Mr. Stanley says, distress must always exist. Have we anything better to oppose to it than our good old-fashioned charity, or some improvement in the poor-laws?'

'My dear Harley,' said Lord Aiden, softly through his smoke-wreaths, 'the monastic orders of the Middle Ages were a new discovery practically. The monasteries,' he went on, turning to Mr. Stanley, 'offered a certain relief to the sufferings of those who were oppressed by society; and you perhaps would say that men in the modern world should aim at finding some substitute for the monasteries.'

'I,' Mr. Stanley began, 'should go even farther than that——' But the musical voice of Lady Chislehurst interrupted him.

'Mr. Carew,' she exclaimed, 'you must please listen to this. If you will allow me to do the intellectual honours of your house for you, I must tell everybody that the meeting of our Society is begun. We are in the middle of it even before we knew that it had opened. Listen, listen. This is our contribution from Rome. Mr. Stanley,' she continued as she settled her voluminous skirts, 'go on. We are atttending.'

Mr. Stanley emitted a little dry laugh. 'I was,' he said, 'merely about to observe to Lord Aiden that though the monasteries in the Middle Ages did much, we should aim at doing relatively even more. My own belief is—and here is an answer to Mr. Harley—that there is being developed in us the consciousness of a new duty—I mean our spiritual duty to the material conditions of the poor, of which in past ages we have been in invincible ignorance.'

'It's all very well,' said Harley, 'for us to talk about this new duty; and I quite agree that the world is growing to feel it. But have we any of us any ideas more practical than those of Foreman as to the means, the machinery, by which to put it in practice?'

'I have one friend,' said Mr. Stanley, with a momentary glance towards Miss Consuelo Burton, 'who has a very definite idea indeed.'

'Hush,' said Lady Chislehurst. 'Attend. Consuelo, tell Mrs. Harley—for you have not told her yet—what your thoughts are on the subject. You need not be shy, for they have been spoken of to the Holy Father; and they will help to show Mrs. Harley what Catholics really are.'

Carew watched the girl as closely as the dusk permitted him. He saw her impatiently turn her head aside; he saw her for a moment bite her lip with annoyance; and then, in a voice half constrained and half mischievous, 'My thoughts,' she said, 'as a Catholic, Lady Chislehurst, are these. Men who are housed like pigs can hardly pray like Christians; and where life is a long flight from starvation, it is not a flight that takes the fugitives towards heaven.'

'Perhaps,' said Mr. Stanley, at once coming to her assistance, 'Miss Consuelo Burton will let me speak instead of her, and explain the idea—it is a very suggestive one—that came into her mind after her visit at Courbon-Loubet. Suppose, then—Mrs. Harley, here is the point that appeals to you—suppose we take these men who are housed like pigs. The increasing masses of them, clustering in huge cities, are the special phenomenon and problem of the modern world, and the Church is interested in them just as much as the State. Of course, for these people spiritually there is hope in the uncovenanted mercy; but our business as Catholics and as practical men is not to trust to the uncovenanted mercy, but to extend the kingdom of the covenanted.'

'Hear, hear!' exclaimed Mrs. Harley, softly.

'This is the idea,' Mr. Stanley went on, 'which, not to mention myself, has impressed itself most strongly on the mind of Miss Consuelo Burton. She feels that sanitary and social work, carried out on some wide and organized plan, is a necessary part of modern religious propagandism; and in case anyone should think such sentiments un-Catholic, I may mention that I have expressed them myself in language quite as emphatic in a short discourse which I submitted lately to the Pope, and which will very shortly, I hope, be published with his sanction.'

'Indeed!' said Lord Aiden. 'I shall read that with interest. But let us by all means hear what the ideas of our young friend here are.' And he laid his hand on the back of Miss Consuelo's chair, as if entrusting the wood to transmit the action to her shoulder.

'Well,' said Mr. Stanley, 'the idea is simply this—and at first sight it will not strike you, perhaps, as so novel as it really is. You have spoken, Lord Aiden, of the monastic system already. The idea I am about to explain is a modification of that system. You all recollect, no doubt, a little economic argument which I had at Courbon-Loubet with that worthy man Mr. Foreman?'

'Yes,' said Mrs. Harley, 'perfectly—every word of it.'

'You recollect, then,' said Mr. Stanley, 'what I told him his error was? I told him that the minority, who, he said, were thieves and marauders—I mean the men who direct and organize industry—I told him that these men seized on the growing wealth which they possess for the plain reason that virtually they created it; and further, that they only created it for the sake of themselves possessing it. The desire to possess it, I urged on him, was a natural appetite, having the same relation to production that hunger has to cooking; and to expect that the talent and astonishing mental activity which on the part of the minority has produced our modern wealth—to expect that this activity will still continue to be developed when its normal stimulus is wholly taken away from it, is to expect of the minority an act of supernatural virtue as unfit for the world at large as the rule of the Trappist cloister. Perhaps you recollect my having said that to Foreman ?'

Several voices murmured 'Yes,' and Mr. Stanley continued.

'I put my criticism in that way without premeditation; but it at once struck Miss Consuelo Burton. It was merely a seed dropped by the wayside; but in her mind it has flowered into this suggestion. The monastic rule, she argues, is not fit for everyone, but it is fit for some, and these the most devoted of mankind. Why, then, should not the old monastic renunciation of riches be revived in the modern world, under the form of a renunciation of profits? If all the directors of industry, the inventors, the sharp men, the men of energy and enterprize, through whose means industry grows in productiveness, would still exert themselves to maintain and increase production, and at the same time forego their claim to the increased products, then, she says—and she is perfectly, she is obviously right — the Socialistic problem would be solved. But, as we said just now, to forego these natural claims would be nothing less than a special monastic virtue of precisely the same character as poverty and celibacy. It is not to be thought of for all ; but, she asks, may it not well be thought of for some?'

'Yes,' said Lady Chislehurst, in a reverie of approbation, casting her eyes down on a small silver crucifix. 'Yes, the point is there.'

'Do you mean,' interposed Harley, ' that some—what shall we say — some railway company should every quarter pay its dividends into the poor-box? I'm not laughing—I'm merely trying to get at the idea.'

' No,' said Mr. Stanley, ' the idea is not that. What has presented itself to the mind of Miss Consuelo Burton is a vision of some new industrial order, or orders, under which the monastic vow of poverty might be applied to our modern factory system. Her notion, in fact, of a monastery or a convent is a modern factory where the hands should be monks or nuns; where the spire should rise side by side with the chimney; and the quiet cloister should refresh the mind after the rattle of wheels, and looms, and belts.'

'That,' said Lord Aiden, in a tone of poetic appreciation, 'makes a really beautiful picture. And when are we to look forward to seeing Miss Consuelo Burton an abbess? But, tell me,' he added, relapsing to the levels of prose, 'how would such an establishment differ from any other co-operative enterprize based on the principle of profit-sharing?'

'Ah,' said Mr. Stanley, 'that is what I am coming to. The profits, of course, instead of going to the capitalists, the manager, and the specially-gifted few, would be the property of the whole body. They would not, however, be divided amongst the workers, and thus take the form of increased wages. That result would stultify the whole scheme. The whole monastic body would live in voluntary poverty—on lower wages, rather on higher wages, than the average worker outside; and all their profits would be set by as a fund to relieve distress, especially such as is caused by commercial crises. In that way the Catholic religion and system would be brought into practical contact with the modern industrial world, and would become a visible part of it. The idea is one—at least I find it so—which becomes more suggestive the more one thinks of it.'

Silence reigned for some moments when Mr. Stanley ceased speaking. At last Mrs. Harley whispered, ' Yes, the idea is beautiful.' And then, with an abruptness which made them all start, Carew, as if continuing some train of unspoken thought, said, 'Charity is far from being their only work. It is not even the chief. Their chief work will be their living example. By the stern simplicity and yet perfect content of their lives, by the decency of their habits despite their utter poverty, they will form a moral leaven amongst the labouring classes at large, and do more than anything I ever had thought imaginable, to give an ideal dignity to our modern factory-labour. Fancy,' he went on, ' over the gate into the factory-yard, if we saw a crucifix placed there with real meaning! And this too—think of this. Here and there some man of high position has renounced his place in the world and adopted the life of a labourer. In the present condition of things such conduct is useless and fantastic; it is very much like madness. But there would be nothing fantastic in it if labour became conventual.'

He ceased as abruptly as he began, and his eyes were turned in the gloom towards the glimmer of Miss Consuelo's dress.

'Well,' said Mr. Stanley, in his most practical and incisive accents, 'you have heard the idea that Lady Chislehurst promised you. I don't know that to-night we can do much towards making it clearer.'

'Anyhow,' said Mrs. Harley, 'you have given us much to think of.'

'And I,' said Carew to himself when his friends had once more left him, 'I might join my life to the life of a woman with thoughts like these, if I had not bound myself by an idle debt to another, from which she—my better angel—would despise me if I released myself.'

CHAPTER VI.

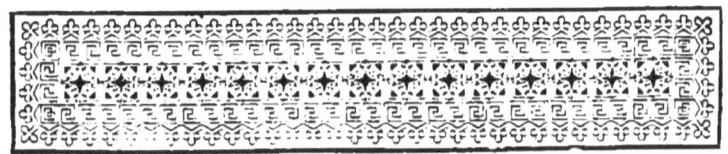E passed the night in restless and almost irritated perplexity. The irritation, however, was a hopeful and healthy sign, for he was next morning in a more vigorous mood, even if not in a happier one. He resolved in a practical way, like a man beset by creditors, to cast up his moral accounts, and examine instead of contemplating his situation.

How did he stand with regard to Miss Capel? That was the great question which he must carefully reconsider. He tried to do this, and indeed he did do it, impartially;

and here is the story which for his own benefit he told himself.

The moment he was free from the spell of the girl's presence, the void left by her absence was suddenly filled to overflowing by a throng of practical interests and entirely alien feelings. On this, his old desire for her, if it did not actually die, became as faint as the moon's disc in daylight, and the evanescence of his attachment for her had paralyzed his power of imagining her attachment to him.

Then he went on to reflect as follows. His forgetfulness of her was not wholly his own fault. She had in many ways laid the foundations of it herself. Never for a moment had she seemed to consider the bare possibility of her freeing herself from her existing engagement. If at times she had yielded tenderly to her inclination for him she recovered herself with ease, and very often with flippancy ; and if he had occasionally wondered since he had left her whether she might not be really unhappy at the loss of him, he had checked the thought as the child of his own vanity.

At last, late in the day, utterly unexpected, her letter had fallen on him like a thunderbolt out of a clear sky, or rather it had been like a dagger stuck suddenly in his heart. After all, he discovered that this girl had felt for him, not only as much as she had seemed to feel, but more ; and when she had seemed to forget those feelings, it turned out that she was only fighting against them. She had been fighting to save herself—fighting helplessly and piteously. And he, he alone, had to answer for all this. He appeared to himself like a man who had been torturing a child for his amusement. In his own eyes he was utterly degraded and humiliated.

Yielding to an impulse that was at first but a selfish longing for distraction, he had sought her society as a kind of mental dram-drinking, and had gradually done his utmost to evoke in her a passion for himself. He dwelt on the phrases he now remembered he had used to her—'life of my life,' 'soul of my soul,' and so forth. And in the light of the self-knowledge that now too late had come to him, he wondered blankly and bitterly at what could have then possessed him. He saw that, all the while he had been allowing this licence to his emotions, he had been doing so comfortably, with the thought at the back of his mind that they would vanish, if necessary, almost as easily as they arose; and he had idly said to himself that the same would hold good with her. And now his position was like that of the Witch of Endor. A spirit of love had indeed arisen in her, but it was a spirit of a different order from the one he had meant to summon. It was a spirit that refused to vanish. It would not even retreat. It stood before him, and overawed him with the sound of its voice. But what was the voice saying?

Here came the hard, the practical, the immediate point which he had to face and decide upon. Was the voice simply upbraiding him, with a resigned and hopeless despondency? Or was it urging him, was it imploring him at once to do something? *Something*! Why not call it by its right name? Was it urging him, before it was too late, to fly to her rescue, and offer his hand and life to her, and save the soul whose whole future he had endangered? Could this really be so? Could that pleasant past, that dream of flowers and poetry, thus rise against him and demand from him this sacrifice?

Again and again he put the question to his conscience, and his conscience seemed to him not like a single councillor, but rather like a cabinet of opposing scruples and excuses which were not able to come to any decision. On one hand it was urged that he was too late already, and that even if he offered himself Miss Capel would not accept him; on the other, that he ought at least to allow her to have the chance; and again, that he also should think of the utter and hopeless shipwreck which he would if he married her be making of his practical life. He was determined, however, to force himself to some resolution; and going to a drawer where Miss Capel's last letter was deposited, he again referred to the date on which it was written, and compared this with the interval which then, she said, separated her from her marriage.

The letter now was at least ten days old. Her marriage when she wrote would take place in three weeks' time. There were accordingly eleven days before him, in which he might give her the opportunity of saving herself from certain misery. She was still at Cannes; and in four-and-twenty hours a letter could reach her, or even he himself. There at any rate was something settled and certain. Should he decide on making, or rather, on risking the sacrifice, he had ample time to do so. He had no excuse on that score. But what then of his conduct to Miss Consuelo Burton? His conversation with Mr. Stanley about her came back to his mind, and he asked his conscience if she also had no claim on him, and if of the two claims hers were not the older.

At last he came to a fixed resolve on one point. He would do something, which though it might prove painful he would do at once, and do bravely and thoroughly. He would seek counsel of Miss Consuelo Burton herself. He would confess everything—the whole of his heart—to her ; he would place his life, his whole future in her hands ; and she should at least choose his road for him, even if she could not travel it by his side.

He had settled this with himself not a moment too soon, for his friends were to come to him for the midday breakfast, and, as it happened, they arrived a little before their time.

Carew's heart began to sink within him ; but during the meal he received a little unintended encouragement. The conversation at first had been but semi-serious ; several allusions, however, had been made to the topic of the previous evening ; and at last Mrs. Harley, in a spirit of friendly banter, said to him, ' Well, and on what do your hopes rest now ? Who is going to save us from ruin and revolution—the new monastic orders, or the old landed families ? '

' Both,' said Carew, laughing, though his

manner was somewhat absent. 'Yes,' he went on, suddenly becoming animated, 'let the new monastic orders do all that we could dream of their doing—and I for one can dream of their doing much—I still hold that if the world is to recover its health again, if there is to be any increase of happiness amongst the bulk of the labouring classes— the classes whose content is the corner-stone of civilization, another thing must revive besides the monastic orders : there must be a revival of class feeling.'

'Surely,' said Harley, laughing, 'we've plenty of that already.'

'Yes,' said Carew, 'of class envy and of class fear, we have. Everyone is either in terror of losing his position, or else angry and sullen at not being able to escape from it. The class feeling I mean is a feeling possible only when classes are acquiesced in as stable and natural institutions, and movement from one to the other is looked upon as only exceptional. For instance, I say this : the healthy ambition of the average country labourer should consist in a desire not to escape from his cottage, but to adorn his cottage with security, content, and affection. His eye should seek the faces of those around him, not the coat-tails of those who are just above him. And as to the aristocracy, their whole life should be guided by a sense of duty to the great multitude that is connected with them by the difference of its lot, not by the sameness of it. It is very possible that I am only a dreamer, but still I cannot help indulging the dream, that the obligation of acknowledged position, that high-breeding, and even family pride, have a mission still in the world, if we only can find it out.'

'My dear Carew,' said Mr. Stanley, putting his hand on Carew's arm, 'feeling as you feel about these gifts and qualities, I should venture to say that in your case they had a mission already.'

Carew rose from the table thinking, ' If this be so, can it really be that I am bound to renounce my talents? '

It was now not long before the moment came for which he had been longing, though at the same time he was dreading it. The party soon, in a somewhat desultory way, proceeded to spread themselves over the villa and the gardens, and without having designed the situation, almost before he had even realized it, he found himself on a terrace alone with Miss Consuelo Burton.

He felt that now or never the bold plunge must be made ; so, beating about the bush as little as possible, he paused in his walk, and leaning against the marble balustrade, gravely raised his eyes to her, and began in this way.

' Do you remember,' he said, ' our conversations at Courbon-Loubet? '

She too paused. She looked him in the face for a moment, and then said simply, 'Yes, I have not forgotten them. Do you think that either of us is any nearer the truth since then?'

'You are,' he said. 'Tell me, do you remember this? You said that in your search for truth you would let me be your helper—that is, if you needed help from anyone.'

'Did I?' she said. 'How long ago was that? Some weeks—I don't think more; but during that time I have become years older.' Then changing her tone, and with a resolute frankness looking at him, 'Yes,' she went on, 'I remember quite well, and I was told directly afterwards that you wanted to help nobody—I mean not in that way.'

'Do you believe that now?'

She merely shook her head.

'And yet,' said Carew, 'it is true; but not in the way you thought it was. I should no longer dare to say that I wanted to help you, for with far more fitness I should ask you to help me. May I,' he went on, seeing that she said nothing, and his voice as he spoke sank and became tremulous, 'may I ask you a few questions?'

'Go on,' she said, 'ask them.'

'Tell me this, then,' said Carew, 'for I trust your judgment. You heard what Mr. Stanley said to me about my mission in life. Do you think it true ? Do you think that it must be really a man's highest duty to consecrate any powers, any external advantages he may be born with, to the service of those who are working and suffering round him ? Do you think that our first debt is due to those rather than to any private creditors on one's conduct, whose claims, perhaps, one may be unable to satisfy without becoming a bankrupt as to all the others ?'

'I think,' she said, 'you must be making

some special allusion, but I do not know to what. I can only answer you generally, and tell you my own feelings. Duties like those you speak of, so it seems to me, differ in proportion to our own powers of seeing them. Some of them, or some forms of them, are more or less like ghosts : they appear to some eyes only ; and those that don't see them of course have no call to follow them. But when once one of these ghosts has appeared to anyone, that person is never the same afterwards. One must try to follow it even though it " lead one to the cliff" like Hamlet's father, or else one's whole life long one will feel one has made " the great refusal." I never asked or prayed to see *my* ghost ; I never went out of my way to think about the poor or about the people ; but I seem to have absorbed like a sponge all I have heard about their lives, or read about them in the newspapers, or seen by chance in the streets or other places. I remember our housekeeper once telling me that cocoa would take the taste of any groceries it was standing near. My thoughts, in the same way, are full of the taste of poverty. I don't try to keep it there, but I can't get rid of it.'

'I,' said Carew, 'like you, have seen the duty you speak of. The same ghost has appeared to both of us. Do you think, then, using your conscience as mine, that no consideration for the mere personal feelings either of myself or of those near me should induce me to surrender my powers of doing this duty effectually?'

She looked at him with an air of perplexity. 'I can only tell,' she said, 'what I feel in the matter myself. Perhaps the time may come when I shall be called on to say good-bye, not merely to luxury, but to the pleasure of books, of poetry, of music—all those refinements with which it is generally thought a duty to pamper oneself; and I suppose in that case I should be called on to starve one whole side of my nature. Perhaps, should the time ever come, I shall be unequal to the sacrifice; but if it is a question of what I ought to do, I feel that for the duty we speak of I ought to renounce everything —the pleasure of self-culture, the pleasure of pleasing those nearest to me.'

'Is it true,' said Carew after a pause, ' that you think of a conventual life for yourself, or at least of keeping yourself for such a life at some future time ? '

She smiled faintly and pensively, and turned her head away from him.

'I don't know,' she said, 'if I am fitted for such a life. I am very worldly in some ways. I hate an ugly hat, or ugly gloves or boots. Though I didn't acknowledge it at Courbon-Loubet, I have almost as much prejudice about birth and family as you have.

I am fastidious about people's manners, and I easily think them common. Oh, and there are other things—perhaps I have no vocation.'

She stopped short suddenly. Carew started and looked at her. Her head was averted, but he could see that her cheek was crimson, and her breast was lifted with a slow and suppressed breathing.

For a moment his voice failed him. He had his heart in his mouth, and a throng of words, like the forlorn hope of an army, seemed to pause, arrested and tremulous, before they broke forth in passion. This instinctive hesitation gave him time to collect himself, and when he spoke it was with a constrained calmness.

'Will you listen,' he said, 'to something I want to tell you? You must see from what I have said already that I am thinking of serious things, and you must see from my speaking about them to you that I look on you as a person who can share, and is now consenting to share, the deepest thoughts of which I am conscious : the thoughts, the feelings—I don't know what to call them—which my soul will live or die by. You will listen to me, won't you ?'

She bent her head as a sign for him to proceed.

'I am going,' he went on, 'to say two things to you ; and do you say nothing—no word—in answer to the first till you have heard the second. We have talked of duty—we have talked of a special duty, which both to you and to me too seems in these days the first duty of all, and alone to give religion a body instead of leaving it merely a sigh. But I know myself so well that I dread this. I am almost certain of this—if left to myself, I shall not cease to think, but I shall never begin to act. If, however, I could find someone who could understand me and would help me—who, by sharing my thoughts and impulses, would strengthen them a thousandfold, and who would make me by her presence incapable of any shameful thought —then, indeed, I might dare to hope that on my death-bed I should be able to say to myself, "I have not lived in vain." Can you imagine, to a soul like mine, any healing, any consolation like this? Consuelo, your name is Consolation—you must know that I speak of you.'

She had not moved. Her eyes had been still averted, but he saw that the colour was still deep in her cheek, and that she was biting her lip hard. At last, when he paused, she turned to him for a single moment, and tears, helpless and uninvited, were filling her dark eyes.

'I have not finished,' he went on, 'and when you hear what remains perhaps you will think that I should not have said what I have said. And yet no; I retract that. I trust you so entirely that I am sure you will not misjudge me. Perhaps when I tell you all I shall lose your respect in one way; but at least you will respect me for having honestly told you. When you went away from Courbon-Loubet—when you said goodbye to me as if I were hardly fit to be spoken to—but I won't talk of that. You know how it all happened.'

'I know,' she whispered.

'When you had gone,' he went on, 'I felt like some criminal. I didn't know what I had done, but I felt as if I must have forged, or committed some murder in my sleep. I seemed to myself to be such an utter outcast that I was grateful to the very dogs when they looked at me and put their paws upon my knee. As to you, I was not angry with you; but it seemed to me as if, of your own free will, you had taken yourself away to some hopeless distance from me, and that I should never be able to see you or come near you again. Well, it so happened that, in those days of my desolation I met with some people of whom I had known something before, though only a little.' And Carew gave a brief account of how he had met the Capels, and of the way in which they had come to stay with him at the château.

'The girl,' he continued, 'was very beautiful, and—will you remember, please, that I am trying to tell the exact truth to you, exactly as I should were this the Day of Judgment? As to my own conduct I am going to palliate nothing. This girl, without any effort at first on my part, seemed to sympathize and be pleased with me. If the very dogs at that time touched me by their friendliness, you may judge the effect on me of this beautiful girl's attention. By-and-by

I realized that I did more than please her, and that I exercised over her a certain sort of attraction, which she made at times a strong effort to resist. Her behaviour in this way puzzled and piqued me; the sense of her beauty grew on me. Let me make no words about it—I began to fall in love with her; and more than that, I determined that she should fall in love with me. As often as I was aware of any resistance on her part I was impelled to do recklessly all I could to overcome it. Little by little she made me the helpless victim of as strong an attraction as any I exercised over her. As for you, you seemed somehow far away from me. I didn't forget you, but I saw you, as it were, in another world through some semi-opaque barrier. It is not very pleasant for me to have to tell you this, but you must see me just as I am. I will have no secrets from you. What do you think of a man with constancy such as mine? What could be the value of anything I could offer you? Are you not shocked—disgusted?'

'Did I not tell you,' she said in a low steady voice, 'that during the past few weeks I have grown older by years? I always understood some things more clearly than some girls. The best constancy in man is a virtue; the best constancy in woman is an instinct. I do not judge you as if I had lived only on romances. Go on—you were in love with her.'

'I must,' said Carew, 'tell you in what way. Her influence on me was that of some drowsy spell. I might have roused myself from it; I ought to have done so: I can only say that I did not. And yet all the while I knew in my heart of hearts that I should wake up one day and find that I had been loving in a dream. That an end of some kind was bound very soon to come I knew for one excellent reason. I found that the person I speak of was actually engaged already, and so far as I could see, she never contemplated breaking off the engagement. From this I drew a conclusion, which does not for a moment excuse me, but with which I soothed my conscience. I concluded that she had the same sense as I had of being in an emotional dreamland, and that she would wake up presently in just the same way as I should. In this, however, I find I have been mistaken. My sin has found me out with a vengeance. I have reason to believe that the feelings which I indulged myself by developing in her, are of a more serious nature than I ever dreamed they could be. Into this I don't think I need go particularly. I need only say that if I leave her to the fate that awaits her I may have to answer for having made wretched, or worse than wretched, a life that but for me and for my conduct might have been happy. There are the facts. My confession is over now. If you had not been what you are I should never have dared tell you. I am not pleading my cause, I am not defending myself. I know too well all that can be said against me. If anything can be said for me, your generosity will say it better than I can.'

There was a long pause, and it seemed to both that they could hear their two hearts beating.

When, however, the painful silence was broken, and it was broken first by Miss Consuelo Burton, her voice was still as quiet and hushed as ever.

'If you married her,' she said, 'if she left the other man, whom I conclude she does not like, for you, should you yourself be happy? Are you fond of her enough for that, or in that way?'

Whilst Carew had been speaking she had remained perfectly motionless, with no sign of feeling except that her cheek had grown pale again, and her eyes, cast down, had been fixed on one particular jasmine flower. 'Go on,' she resumed. 'Answer me. I may be able by-and-by to advise you.'

The phrase, chilly but kind, cut Carew to the heart. She seemed already to be speaking to him from the hopeless distance of a convent.

'Listen,' he replied, 'and you shall have my whole confession. You have asked me a question which refers to myself simply—to my own lot, not that of another. I seemed at the time, under the influence of the person we speak of, to be entering, as it were, some terrestrial paradise where all life moved to some dreamy imploring music, where the holiest flower of the soul was love for the sake of love. I do not mean love as opposed to duty, but love considered as the sum and measure of duty. Well, let me tell you what in my sober waking moments I believe about myself. I believe that life, unless I sank into an idle dream again, could never for me, for my own soul, be tolerable, if devoted merely to an affection for its own sake, no matter how beautiful. Indeed, such an affection, unless it mixed itself with my principles of action and sent its pulses through all the veins of my being, of my thoughts, of my intellect, of my most strenuous moral promptings, would soon cease to be an affection at all, and would become merely a burden. In the case of the person I speak of I am certain that this would happen. The ideas of duty and usefulness which, if I am really to live at all, must be my life, are to her mind wholly incomprehensible. As Mr. Stanley would say, she is in invincible ignorance of them.'

Carew paused, and then suddenly went on again. 'This,' he said, 'is owing to no fault of hers. She has none of the ideas which animate you and me. She has been born and brought up in a different world from ours; and these ideas are as strange to her as the Chinese language. By birth and by education she is a foreigner. Miss Burton, I must tell you one thing more. I had forgotten it till this moment, but I must tell it you, for perhaps you will think that it helps to warp my judgment. If I marry a foreigner the bulk of my fortune goes from me. Were I not in the position I am I could easily bear that; but this loss of fortune would mean for me the entire surrender of our old family property; it would mean the handing over to others the care and interest of those whom I else might benefit, the desertion of an order I would willingly die defending, and the throwing away of that power and responsibility which my best ambition is to use, and to use for good. My own feelings, then, are these : whatever value I might set on the affection in question, however urgent might be my duty to adhere to it, adhesion to that duty would and must mean for me a practical renunciation of nearly all others. Whether, as a fact, this affection still continues to influence me, I think you need not ask. To deny a feeling to which one has once owned, when the person who excited it has done nothing to deserve ill of one, goes to one's heart as an act of treachery. If the thing has happened it has happened, but one may be spared speaking about it.'

Miss Consuelo Burton here turned towards him with a slow melancholy movement, and looked him in the face with eyes that were now quite tearless. She seemed by her helpless silence to be expecting him to say more.

'Do you understand,' he went on, 'what it is that I wish to know? She, unless something intervenes to prevent it, will be married in a fortnight's time to a husband she does not care for. I do not know if, under any circumstances, she would break this marriage off; but I do know that, owing to me, it has become hopelessly distasteful to her. Is it my duty to offer myself to her unreservedly, so that if she choose to accept me she may? I ask you this because I feel that I should be nearer you if I left you for the sake of duty, than if, concealing the truth, I won you and possessed you in spite of it.'

'You must let me think,' she said. 'I will tell you to-morrow evening. Listen,' she exclaimed, 'the others are coming this way!' And with a violent effort changing her whole manner, and forcing her lips to wear a conventional smile, 'Come,' she said, 'let us go and meet them. We have talked of this long enough; and you promised that this afternoon you would take them all to some place—where was it? I can remember nothing.'

CHAPTER VII.

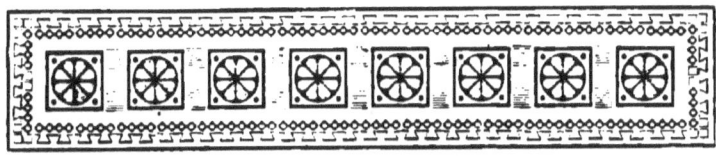AREW, having made his confession, felt in one way more at his ease; though it was the ease combined with the prostration that succeeds some operation of surgery. He was able, however, during the rest of the day to speak to Miss Consuelo Burton without any signs of embarrassment. Indeed, his manner to her was such, and such also was hers to him, as to give Mr. Stanley the impression that a happy understanding was being arrived at by them. He little knew the perplexity and the apprehension that were really lying on each of them like

a heavy dead weight, or how each felt that before another day was over they might be face to face, not with union, but separation.

The afternoon was occupied with a distant excursion by boat, in which all the party joined with the exception of Lady Chislehurst. She went back by herself for a few hours to Baveno, in order to meet her bishop— the Bishop of Wigan and Lancaster—a prelate who had been but lately appointed to his see, and to whom she conceived she could give many hints of importance. When she returned to the Island for dinner the others had not yet arrived; so, following an instinct which very rarely deserted her, and which she had exhibited with such zeal during her visit at Courbon-Loubet, she summoned a servant and asked to be shown the chapel. Of its own style, that of the late Renaissance, it was really a fine specimen, florid with marble and with gilding, and glowing with gorgeous frescoes. It was seated for several hundred worshippers; there was an apparently beautiful organ; and Lady Chislehurst learned that when there was any service the steward of the property—an accomplished musician—was the organist. The twilight prevented her inspection being very minute, but she seemed to have seen enough to be satisfied in a high degree; and when the others at last arrived, they found her in a state of unusual pleasure and excitement.

During dinner the cause of it was explained—the cause, or rather the causes. In the first place, she had had a long conversation with the Bishop, and had told him a variety of things with regard to the poor of the north-west of England, which, so she said, he was exceedingly glad to learn. Then, whilst this interview was going on, who should be announced but one of her atheistic professors, who supplemented his lectures at the Royal Institution by an occasional service at the Positivist Church in Bloomsbury! 'It was charming,' she said, 'to see the Bishop tackle him. The whole thing was done with such dignity and such perfect charity. I only wish Mr. Stanley could have been there too; for what do you think, Mr. Stanley, the Professor was good enough to tell us? So far as the Church's practical teaching went, he quarrelled with it, he said, upon one point only, and that point, if you please, was this. The Church regards sin as an offence against God and against our own souls; whereas the cardinal doctrine in what he called scientific morals is "that sin is simply an offence against society, and regarded as anything else is a mischievous and complete illusion."'

Everyone was astonished that Lady Chislehurst had such patience with error as even to state calmly so monstrous a doctrine as this; but what caused even more astonishment was the fact that she smiled graciously as she did so, and actually seemed to dwell on the recollection of its apostle with complaisance. The explanation of the wonder, however, presently came to light. 'The Professor,' she went on to say, 'found me talking to the Bishop about the poor, and that gave him occasion to allude to the view I have just mentioned. The Bishop, you know, delights in arguing with freethinkers, and has had many a battle-royal with the Professor before; and now, the moment the vexed question was touched upon, what should you think he said? He said, "If you want to compare your religion with Catholicism, you should talk to Mr. Stanley; or, if you can't do that, you should read what he is about to publish." And then he went on to tell us of many things which the Holy Father had said about this very Discourse, Mr. Stanley, of which you were speaking to us this morning. Well, do you know what I did? I told the Professor that, if I could possibly arrange it, there should be Benediction in this chapel to-morrow, and that Mr. Stanley should give us a short sermon upon the very point that was at issue.'

Carew looked across the table at Miss Consuelo Burton, in remembrance of a look which, on a similar occasion, had passed between them at dinner at Courbon-Loubet; but the slight smile that was again exchanged between them had little mirth in it, and no mockery. Even the others, though experiencing the peculiar pleasure which titillates the mind when anyone does anything specially characteristic, were inclined to hear Lady Chislehurst's scheme with interest.

'You must remember, Mr. Stanley,' she

went on, seeing that he did not speak, 'that you are a member of our Society for the discussion and discovery of truth; and I think you owe it to all of us, merely on that ground, to let us have the benefit of your wisdom at this unexpected meeting. If you will do what I suggest I can answer for it that the Professor will be present, and he will bring with him no less a person than Mr. Humbert Spender, who, as the Bishop said to me afterwards, has, of all unbelieving philosophers, done most harm to the cause of Truth.'

Mr. Stanley was quite silent for a moment or two, and his face seemed to have less expression than usual. The reason was that, much as he respected Lady Chislehurst, he could not help, as has been said before, being amused at her, and he was now suppressing a smile at her ultra-episcopal activity. No sooner, however, had he quieted his rebellious muscles, than he said, with perfect gravity:

'It is hardly fair on a preacher to ask, at a minute's notice, for a philosophical sermon. Pious advice, no doubt, we can always give; but arguments are things whose power of touching others depends much on their careful and prepared arrangement; and the best reasoner, if he has to act in a hurry, may hardly be able to be more cogent than the worst. My notes, however, I think are in such order that I might put together, into the form of a suitable sermon, a few of the main points to which I conclude the Bishop alludes, and about which I certainly did have some conversation with His Holiness.'

'I'm sure you could do so, Mr. Stanley,' Lady Chislehurst exclaimed with enthusiasm. 'Think what a blessing such a sermon might be, if only heard by men when in a mood that laid them open to conviction.'

'A modern philosopher,' said Mr. Stanley,

'is, I am afraid, not so easily converted. But it can do him no harm to hear the opposite side of the question.'

'Well,' said Lady Chislehurst to Carew as, at the close of the evening, they were all preparing to re-embark for Baveno, 'I will let these gentlemen know about to-morrow's service, and I've not the least doubt that they will be part of our congregation.'

CHAPTER VIII.

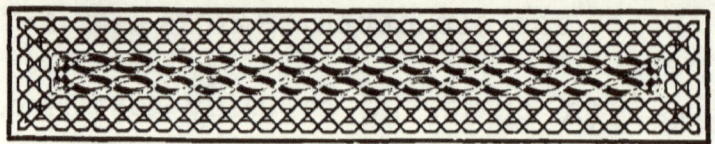HE following morning the Harleys, Lord Aiden, and Mr. Stanley appeared at the Island, during the morning, as they had done before; but there were no Miss Burtons and there was no Lady Chislehurst. Lady Chislehurst would not come till the afternoon, being busy at Baveno with beating up a congregation; whilst the eldest Miss Burton, who had been nursing a slight cold, thought it best to wait and come over with her; and both her sisters decided to do the same.

To Carew this was half a relief and half

a disappointment. As the hour drew near when he was to receive an answer the sense of suspense became more and more pressing, and produced, as is common in such cases, a miserable mixture of exhaustion and utter restlessness.

The day wore slowly on, and the afternoon was maturing, when at last the chapel bell began a monotonous tinkle, and two boats could be seen making their way towards the Island. Carew, glad of anything that demanded exertion, went down to meet them. His own friends had just landed when he arrived, and Lady Chislehurst, like an angel at the gate of Paradise, was watching the debarcation from a second boat of a party of men, with a lady or two, who, she felt persuaded, were all of them on the eve of conversion. She at once introduced to Carew the Professor and the Philosopher—both of them men with a certain grim refinement in their faces, and a mixed air in their dress of deference for convention and contempt of it. The others she merely included in a gracious and comprehensive smile, naming Carew to them, who replied by raising his hat, and at once proceeded to lead the way to the Villa. He had no opportunity, even had he desired one, of exchanging more than a moment's greeting with Miss Consuelo Burton till they were all of them passing into the chapel down a long corridor, and even then there was time for only a single sentence. It so happened that she was walking behind the others, and when, on arriving at the chapel-door, Carew stood holding aside a curtain, she turned to him as she passed, with eyes as frank as a sister's, and yet with a something in them which a sister's could never have, and said :

'I will tell you this evening what yesterday I promised I would tell you.'

A few minutes later the service had begun, and the representatives of modern thought were wondering when it would end. To their clear and masculine intelligences it was indeed a melancholy thing to see men and women in this grand and scientific century bowing to a Power who was nothing but a nursery dream, gravely lighting ridiculous rows of candles, and asking the heroine of a nursery fable to pray for them; whilst the whole ceremony was led by a man who, though they had reason to believe him a sane and even accurate thinker, was now posing before them dressed up like a harlequin. They sniffed the incense as though it were an effluvium from some moral sewer; and the note of reverence and contrite humility which, in the music and the immemorial Latin, sounded through the whole liturgy, was to their ears as irrational as a chorus of cats at midnight. They bore their trial, however, with a very creditable patience ; and at last it came to an end, and Mr. Stanley mounted the pulpit.

A perfect silence at once reigned through the chapel. There was not a whisper, not a foot nor a book was shuffled.

'I will take,' he began, with an absence of conventionality, which at once fixed and increased the curious expectation of his hearers, 'I will take for my text these verses from the General Epistle of St. James.

' " Go to now, ye rich men, weep and howl for the miseries that shall come upon you. Your riches are corrupted, and your garments are moth-eaten. Your gold and silver is cankered, and the rust of them shall be a witness against you, and ye shall eat your flesh as it were fire. . . . Behold the hire of the labourers who have reaped down your fields, which is of you kept back by fraud, and crieth ; and the cries of them which have reaped are entered into the ears of the Lord of Sabaoth.

'"If a brother or sister be naked, and destitute of daily food, and one of you say unto them, Depart in peace, be ye warmed and filled; notwithstanding ye give them not those things needful to the body, what doth it profit?

'" To him that knoweth to do good, and doeth it not, to him it is sin."

'I take,' proceeded Mr. Stanley, 'these verses for my text because I can think of no others that deal so directly with the heart of that special subject which I have been asked to speak about this afternoon. That subject is familiar, I believe, to all who are now listening to me. It is the chief subject which divides modern thought, and you all entertain about it certain special doubts and opinions. To make clearness doubly clear, I will define it in few words, so that you all may see at starting that you and I have the same things in our minds.

'The subject, then, is the nature of virtue, or duty, or goodness, or whatever we like to call the conduct and the moral condition which is held to be most desirable and most admirable in a man and in a citizen. And this virtue—pray remember this, for the whole discussion hinges on it—we have to look at in two lights; first, as conduct, which we desire that citizens should practise; and, secondly, as conduct which citizens can be induced to practise. Why do we wish them to be virtuous? How are they to be persuaded to be virtuous? For, as we all know, it is not easy to be so.

'These two questions are at the bottom of all human problems, not for the Christian world only, but equally for those who cast all religion aside and only busy themselves with political and social improvement. And they require discussion mainly for this reason, that at the present day two answers are offered to them which are thought to be, and which certainly seem to be, contradictory.

'The first answer is an answer we have inherited from our fathers. It is the traditional answer of the Church and of the Age of Faith, and is associated with prayers, sacraments, dogmas, and so forth. The second is supposed to be the great discovery of the age of Science and of Reason.

'I will sum them up both briefly. The first is, that virtue and duty have for their object God, and that our inducement to practise them is the desire to please God and the fear of offending Him. The second answer is that their object is our fellow-man and the health of the social organism; whilst our inducement to practise them is in part the constant prompting or teasing of the tribal instinct, or conscience, and in part our own sympathies, and dread of the disapproval of others, aided by a glow of emotion consequent on the contemplation of idealized Humanity. I presume that you desire me to contrast these two answers, and show you how, as a Catholic, I would either vindicate the former against the latter, or else reconcile the two.

'Let me begin, then, with the second answer—the answer universally given by that modern science which all over the world is said to be supplanting with its simple and demonstrated truths the misleading fables and superstitions of what is commonly called religion. For I have something very decided to say to those who consider this answer satisfactory. I have to say to them, deniers of Christianity as they are, that I not only think their answer has strong claims on our attention, but, within limits, I think it entirely true.

' To show you that I speak of it with

my eyes open, I will state it a little more at length. The scientific moralist of to-day, then, tells us that an act is virtuous because in proportion as such acts are practised the sum of human happiness is maintained or increased; and that an act is evil or sinful, not because our own souls are sullied by it, but because in proportion as such acts are practised sorrow and suffering eventually develop themselves amongst others. One of the most popular and gifted exponents of this theory—I am referring to George Eliot—has explicitly contrasted, as objects and ends of virtue, personal perfection and holiness, which is pointed out as a false object, with " those material processes by which the world is kept habitable "—these latter being held up as the true object; or, to quote a more comprehensive phrase from the same authority, virtue refers and only can refer to, is tested and only can be tested by, its reference to " that great cause by which suffering is to be made to cease out of the world." Thus, the only sin which we can commit against ourselves consists in making ourselves less efficient members of society; and the whole body of acts which we call sins generally would cease to be sins, would be virtuous or else indifferent, if other human beings would thrive no worse in consequence of them. This theory, it is claimed by those who support it, sets virtue on a solid and scientific basis; and by freeing it from its supposed connection with a fantastic and unreal object, makes it incalculably more efficacious in promoting its object in reality.

'I think that, so far as such a matter can be explained in a few words, I have described this theory fairly, and shown that I appreciate what are its salient points. And I repeat, what has possibly been a surprise to some of you, that within limits I think it entirely true, and I think it not only true, but a truth newly discovered. I will only in passing make one criticism, which I shall return to by-and-by, but which at present I will simply indicate. I wish to say that there is a certain class of acts, of forbearances, and conditions of the soul, which the Church and religious people generally regard as virtues, but which this theory can neither explain, enjoin, or make room for. The state called holiness is an example of the virtues I refer to, or rather, it may be said to be a name that comprises all of them. But I merely mention this point as one I shall recur to by-and-by. For the present I waive it. I will put these virtues aside, as though they were not virtues at all, and speak merely of those that are left, as if they were the only virtues existing for us: and they do indeed comprise by far the larger part of them.

'With regard, then, to this great body of

practical virtues, such as honesty, uprightness, temperance, justice, self-control, unselfishness—with regard, I say, to this great body of virtues, and the moral code that enjoins them, I fully and frankly admit, as a Catholic and a Catholic priest, that the modern explanation of them is not only ingenious but true. I am prepared to admit that the test and the justification of virtue is its tendency to maintain and promote the general well-being of the social organism—the improvement and perpetuation of this human race of ours on the surface of this planet. I say I admit this explanation. I do more than admit it: I welcome it, and I do so in spite of a consideration which some of you might perhaps think would stagger me. I told you that I recognized it as not only true but new—a new discovery. I recognize further that the discovery has been made outside the Church, and mainly by men hostile to the Church, and I do not welcome it one whit the less for that.

'Let me ask you to bear this last statement of mine in your minds—a startling statement to non-Catholics, coming from a Catholic priest—whilst I make what at first may strike you as a fantastic and meaningless digression.

'The doctrine of Transubstantiation, as taught by the Catholic Church, is regarded generally by the non-Catholic world as nothing more than an arbitrary and superstitious paradox. Most of those, however, who are now listening to me are, probably, aware that this doctrine, whether true or false, involves a train of reasoning of the most close and elaborate kind; in fact, that it implies and depends upon certain of the philosophic conclusions of the most commanding and most comprehensive thinker that ever lived. It implies and it depends upon certain philosophic conclusions of Aristotle. The same may be said of other ideas and doctrines, which have been either formally enunciated or are generally held by the Church; but this, of Transubstantiation, is enough to illustrate the fact I am going to dwell upon. It illustrates the fact which to the Protestant world may seem curious, that the philosophic system of a heathen philosopher forms an integral part of Catholic Christianity. Yes, let me say it again; the laborious conclusions of one whom none of the Apostles had even heard of; whose name is never mentioned in Gospel, in Epistle, or in Creed—one who himself knew nothing of God the Son, or of God the Father—the views, the conclusions of this heathen amongst the heathens, are now living parts of the body of the Catholic Church—bone of its bone, flesh of its sacred flesh.

'I must further add this. Aristotle's influence over Christian thought dates not from the Apostolic, not even from patristic times, but from the Middle Ages. The Church remained for centuries altogether unconscious of a body of intellectual beliefs which, in the fulness of time, it recognized as involved in, and as essential to, its teaching.

'Perhaps now you realize why I have thus digressed. The relation of the Catholic Church to the philosophy of Aristotle is the type of her relation to all thought and all discovery that is outside herself. Whether truth is discovered within her fold or without it matters nothing to her. Just as in Nature she sees one revelation of God, so does she see another in the heart and in the intellect of man; and just as she interprets the truths which the Heavens declare, so does she take into herself and assimilate the truths which human society discovers. She may not do this at the first moment of their discovery, for the process of assimilation is gradual; but the Holy Spirit, the soul of the Mystical

Body, the "*forma corporis*," as St. Thomas calls the soul—the Holy Spirit knows its own times and seasons, and the assimilation takes place at last. The truth which at this moment the Church is beginning to assimilate is, in my judgment, that modern theory of virtue by which its own authors conceive that the theory of the Church will be superseded.

'Now we come to the point where I and these modern thinkers part company. I believe that so far is their theory from superseding that of the Church, that it is the Church alone which can make their theory practicable. In the temple of the Church there is a vacant place waiting for it, and in that place it will help to build up the fabric; but, taken by itself, as it now stands, it is like a carved stone lying useless in an Egyptian quarry.

'Such is my belief; and I shall now explain it. Virtue, as we all know, is not only not coincident with our natural impulses, but one of its great characteristics is that it constantly runs counter to them. Conscience, therefore, which we may call the spokesman, the steward, the factor, for virtue, must justify virtue in a way which shall satisfy the demands of the intellect—the demands of the intellect in its most serious and most searching mood. Now conscience, according to the theory we are discussing, justifies virtue, as we have seen, by pointing to its connection— a connection which I assume to be demonstrated—with the general well-being of the race, or, if we like to use a sonorous and popular phrase, the collective well-being of humanity.

'So far so good. So far conscience would be right; but if this were its last word, if it had nothing further to add, I maintain that it would have been right in vain. Here I part company with the discoverers of the modern theory. I maintain that the well-being of this perishing human race, regarded by itself, and apart from any further beliefs about it, is not an object which can so present itself to the heart or mind as to force any constant, any general self-sacrifice for the sake of it. It is not an idea on which the heart or mind can permanently or generally rest satisfied.

'The ordinary duties and the ordinary forbearances of the day no doubt become easy to us by habit and education; but for anything beyond these, when there is anything hard to be done, anything delightful or anything alluring to be resisted, above all, when any continuous meaning and hope is sought for in life, habit is not enough. We want to know clearly on what this meaning depends, and to see that the object which our struggles are to subserve is satisfactory. The intellect, as it were, goes into retreat; fixes itself on this question, broods over it, tears it to pieces, does all it can to see it as it really is, free from all illusions. And I say again, that, when submitted to this criticism, the welfare of the race, of humanity, of the Social Organism, of the human inhabitants of this planet, is an idea which can permanently satisfy neither the heart nor the intellect of man.

'Perhaps for a generation, to those who have first seized on it, it may seem satisfactory, because it has the glow and the bloom of novelty. But the bloom will not stand the friction of persistent thought, which the mind instinctively will be always longing to bear on it; and by-and-by a more sober and far keener judgment will supervene. To the eye of reason, unaided by faith, but aided on the other hand more and more by science, this planet we inhabit will seem more and more insignificant, the human beings who swarm on it more and more microscopic, their duration as a race more ephemeral, their collective destiny more indifferent. The little circle of personal pleasures and appetites, embraced by the glance of selfishness, and measured by the standards of selfishness, may indeed retain its hold on men. But this is the sphere not of virtue but of the exact reverse of virtue. Virtue can only be ours, according to the scientific theory, through our rising out of this sphere, taking a wider view, and contemplating the race as a whole; and that object of contemplation, unless we have faith to aid us, the more familiar we grow with it will grow less and less—I don't say only less impressive, but less—interesting. Contemplation for the scientific moralist will have an effect the exact reverse to what from time immemorial it has had upon all believers. To the believer the withdrawal of the soul from the vain interests of the world opened a vision of the deeper realities behind the world. To the unbeliever this same earnest withdrawal may indeed show him that the world is vain; but it will show him that anything beyond the world is colder and vainer still. No idea more depressing, more hopeless, more ludicrously miscalculated to evoke heroism, or to curb passion, can possibly be imagined than the human race as a whole, as it shows itself to the eye of reason unaided by faith.

'But to change listlessness into life, to change contempt into reverence, to fire the lukewarm soul with the spirit that makes martyrs, one thing only is needful—one thing suffices. That is a belief in God, and the human soul as related to God. I am not referring at present to the personal desire for heaven or the personal fear of hell. I am not referring to that at all. I am referring simply to the effect of these beliefs on that Idea which the thinkers of the day present us with—the Idea of the human race as a single organic Whole, to which we owe all our duties. It is to that that I am calling your attention. I am thinking at present of no other point but that. That is the point to which all I have said already has been leading up. Let me ask you to listen to me earnestly.

'Duty to the race, as a substitute for duty to God, is, I say, worth nothing; it means nothing. But duty to the race regarded in a very different way, regarded as a new and more definite interpretation of our duty to God, is a conception which to us as Catholics is of the very highest importance. It does not supersede that duty ; no : it helps us to understand its meaning and its depth more fully. I tell you I sit at the feet of our modern teachers ; I accept the good of the social organism as the formal test of virtue ; I admit that virtue is relative to that good altogether ; I mean by this good of the social organism, the amelioration of the material condition of each individual life ; but I declare that such amelioration can present itself to us as a duty, so as to satisfy the intellect and take hold of the heart, only in virtue of a living belief on our part, that it somehow represents the will and purpose of God, and points to issues which reason cannot even guess at. The perpetuation of the race, so long as the planet is habitable— which it will be for only a moment longer—a moment only as compared with the life of the universe—this object, in itself so unsatisfactory, becomes transfigured when we believe that God wills it ; when we know that some purpose, behind the veil, is subserved by it ; and when we realize that virtue, though its formal test may be its social results merely, is in itself, is in its essence, a co-operation with God's will—the will of Him who holds the stars in the hollow of His hand, and whom the heaven of heavens cannot contain—to whom the earth is no larger than an ant-hill, but to whom an ant-hill is large as all infinity.

'Once let the scientific moralist see his creed thus affiliated to Christianity, and whether or no he can believe the Christian region true, he will see that, if true, his theory clings to it, and coheres with it, and coalesces with it, and acquires a something which it never had before. On the other hand, let the Catholic and the Christian once see his own religion assimilating this scientific theory, and he will see a practical relationship, which he may have been tempted to doubt of, suddenly reveal itself between that religion and the special problems of the day—between the religion of the ages of faith and the problems of the age of railways. He will hear the voice of the Catholic Church telling him as clearly as any scientific theorist or lecturer, as clearly as philanthropist or republican reformer, that it is not enough to conceive of virtue as referring to our own souls' salvation or that of the souls of others. He will see that because it does refer to the spiritual condition of others it refers equally to their material condition also. He will see this, and seeing it, he will find that the echoes of the Mass and the confessional follow him, and mix naturally with the clatter of omnibuses.

'Let me dwell a little longer on this. I can hardly leave it. A man's home, his family, his means of livelihood—these are the chalice which holds the sacramental wine of his life, and if we allow the chalice to be soiled or leaky the wine will be defiled or wasted. God wills that it should not be wasted; and though even in this case, there is hope that in His uncovenanted mercy He will gather up the scattered drops, yet, so far as we are concerned wasted it most certainly is: and if so, for that waste we—we—are responsible. If we are responsible when we make one brother offend by tempting him, we are equally responsible if we make him offend by leaving him in those wretched conditions where nothing but offence is possible. This truth in its fulness is only now dawning upon the world. It is the special revelation vouchsafed to us in this epoch of scepticism. In former ages the world was blind to it, and so, let us hope, it did not know sin. Now the Church is receiving the revelation. She that assimilates all things that are of God, no matter by what channels they are sent to her, she is assimilating this new truth—her spiritual duty to the material condition of men; and just at the time when the nations are declaring her to be dying, she against whom the gates of Hell shall never prevail is giving to the nations a new sign of life.

'I have no wish to enter into the vague land of prophecy; but I feel myself not to be talking as a prophet, but as an ordinary man making an ordinary forecast, when I say that new saints such as St. Bernard, St. Dominic, and St. Francis will find in the near future a new field opened to them; and for us who are not saints the same field will be open also—the field of sanitary and of social improvement, the field of trade, of factory labour, and the capitalistic system. Through all the sights and sounds of the present day, through the noise of the terminus, through the hoardings covered with advertisements, we shall, with no sense of incongruity, discern the vision of God; and when, tired at night, we are closing our eyes in sleep, we may feel that we have laid our most material labours on His altar. Christ, when on earth, learnt literally a material handicraft. The mystical Body of Christ, which is on earth still, will not disdain the path that has been trodden by the Son of the Carpenter.

'And now I am going to make an abrupt transition. Having said thus much of that great body of virtues which modern science has analyzed, and with results so important, I return to those other virtues which, for argument's sake, I left out of count at starting: those virtues which I said the scientific moralist could never explain, and which, perhaps, he does not consider to be virtues at all— I return to these; and having spoken of these I shall conclude. In speaking of them, what I trust to show you is this: not that their object is God, and our own souls as related to God—for that, though true, hardly requires proof—but that, so far are they from not being virtues from the utilitarian standpoint, so far are they from being a superfluous addition to those virtues whose object is the welfare of society, that it is through them and through our possession of them only that the utilitarian virtues become in any way binding on us, that we acquire grace to practise them consistently, or find in practising them any sure comfort.

'I say, then, once more that the service of the human race is a satisfactory service—satisfying the entire emotional and intellectual needs of man—only because the social welfare of that race is the will of God. Thus duty consists in co-operating at all costs with that will; and very often the cost is heavy indeed. Here, then, comes the crucial practical question. What consideration or motive is to nerve us to bear that cost? One thing, and one thing alone; that is the love of God. And now consider this. There are many states of the heart, as you all know, in which the love of anything remote from the world of sensual pleasure is impossible; in which any ideal aim, in which any spiritual conceptions, seems to us like a dream. The heart, then, is like a mirror which has been painted on, and which cannot reflect the sun; or like one of the contacts in an electrical apparatus which has become dirty and will not allow the current to pass through it. In contradistinction to a state of the heart like this, is that state, or those states, which we call by the name of holiness. Holiness consists in the cleansing of this mirror, or this electrical contact, so that our hearts may receive the vision of God, may be conscious of the current of His love, and may themselves be moved towards Him. It is only in virtue of their being in this state, or of their approaching it, that we can feel the love which enables us—which alone enables us—to do and to suffer all things; which alone will give a value in our eyes to all our social activities, in face of the apparent failure surely in store for so many of them; for it will teach us to lay them in faith as an oblation at His feet.

'I speak of practical failure, and I do so

with deliberation ; because if there is one lesson taught us by all human experience, all human experience teaches us this—that partial failure is sure to crown every effort ; and however we struggle to alleviate misery, though we may do much, we shall never make earth a paradise. There is no Utopia, there is no new Atlantis, there is no Icaria for us here. The knowledge that this is so—and no enthusiasm, however strong, can in the long run shield us from the knowledge—would be enough to daunt us, and would be sure to daunt us, if we did not know one thing : that behind this apparent failure there is a Power that judges our acts, not by what to our eyes they seem to have accomplished, but by what He sees they aimed at. It is in this we have the indescribable and unfathomable comfort of knowing in faith that a life which in its visible results is only a saddening failure, a forlorn repulse, is not for that reason reckoned of less value when cast into God's treasury.

'Oh, my brethren!' exclaimed the speaker, breaking for the first time into the impassioned tone of a preacher, 'when we consider the millions of human beings around us now, and the countless millions that will come after us, when we consider this mass in its overwhelming aggregate, how little can be done for it by the greatest of men singly! How shall we encourage and comfort ourselves in the face of this paralyzing, this insidious thought, when we are asked to sacrifice things that are much to us for the sake of what to this huge mass is so little? We can only do so by the divine paradox, the holy and saving teaching which the Church alone can give, which to the Positivists is a stumbling-block, and to men of science foolishness, that it is more important to every man that he should do his utmost for humanity, than it can be for humanity that any one man should do his utmost for it.

'And that importance to the individual lies in this. Bear with me, such of you as think the soul and its immortality a fiction— bear with me whilst I address you all as though it were the central fact of life! That importance to the individual lies in this: that he owes his soul to God as an everlasting debt; he owes to God this soul's submission to God's will, and its co-operation with God's will; and he is bound to keep this soul pure and holy because without such virtues he is unable to see God, or do the work God wills in this stony social vineyard. Remember this —I beseech you remember this: in exact proportion as these virtues are cultivated does the Divine Vision become clearer and the motive power of social virtue grow in strength. Hence,' Mr. Stanley proceeded, and his voice, which still retained its earnestness, seemed suddenly to soften into a note of pleading personal solicitude, 'hence we see how the reception of the Lord's Body, together with the preparation needful for receiving it worthily, fits us, not only for the repose of heaven, but for work in the modern world. The same, too, may be said of another Sacrament—the Sacrament of Marriage. Marriage, as every priest knows, as every man of the world knows, cannot in every case—not only is not, but cannot—be a perfect union. The circumstances do not admit of it. But there can be, and there are, good marriages, just as there are good communions. There are marriages in which the intellect and the sympathy of the husband and wife so unite as to direct their two lives with a doubled intelligence and ardour to their work in the world, and with a devotion doubled in clearness and in steadfastness to offer that work to God.

'Sacramental, too, in their nature, are those external advantages which raise the minority of the world above the majority. And this observation brings me to the last thing I have to say to you. You will see that throughout my address to you, I have been addressing myself to those who by position, by intellect, by education, are placed more or less above the ordinary level of mankind. To the labouring classes themselves there is a similar message to be given; but I am referring now to the others, because to their class you belong who are listening to me. You are those to whom much has been given. You are those of whom much will be required. And to you I would say—specially to such of you as have not only the gifts of knowledge and intellect, but also the advantages of material riches and the prestige of inherited positions—to you I would say, Think how, in the light of what I have just been urging, your own responsibility becomes more pressing and definite. What the chisel and the trowel are to the labourer, your wealth and your social example are to you. Should it be God's will that in the hidden course of the future these tools should be taken from you, you will use whatever tools may be put into your hands instead; but so long as they remain yours do not be ashamed of them, do not think, like cowards, of casting them away from you. Do not hide your talents in a napkin through any fear of other men's envy or your own heavy responsibility. Use these splendid tools: your duty is to use them. And if you do, in all human probability you will be confirmed in their possession here, as well as meriting the reward of God hereafter.

'But suppose that, as I hinted, they should be taken away from you, through God's permission in the course of social change, and should your practical power for good thus seem to be crippled—suppose you should lose wealth and consideration, or that any one of you should lose the comfort and the spiritual help of human love, you must not for that reason petulantly cease to struggle. In that case turn to Christ, and think of His social condition. He had neither wealth, nor temporal power, nor a wife's companionship. But He showed Himself to us divested of all such helps and advantages, not that He might teach us to think lightly of them if they are given to us, but that He might teach us that our want of them is no excuse for our refusing to do our duty; that we should none of us say, " Because I am poor, because I am solitary, for these reasons, Lord, I am unable to follow Thee." '

CHAPTER IX.

THE strangers from Baveno, as soon as the service was over, lingered at the door to address a few words to Carew; and, when they had done this, they also expressed a wish to thank Mr. Stanley for the sermon he had just given them, at the same time saying that they would not undertake to criticize it except by praising the courtesy and moderation of its tone. They were not, however, allowed to go without the offer of some slight refreshment, and Carew also took them through part of the Villa and the garden. By the time he had seen them into their boat the daylight had almost faded, and the first bell rang as a warning of approaching dinner. The decisive moment now could not be long postponed. Dinner was the only event that stood between him and it, and it may be easily imagined that, as he did his duties as host, he did not distinguish himself by any great vigour of appetite.

One remark during dinner, and one remark only, roused him. This was a question put to him by Lady Chislehurst—the same question he had himself put to the boatman —as to who lived in the villa that had once been Madame de Saint Valery's. It appeared that prior to their coming over to chapel she and the rest of her party had been for a row on the lake, and this villa had excited the admiration of all of them. Carew said with constraint, that he knew as little about it as they did; and the next moment, with an almost painful start, he found Lady

Chislehurst telling him that they had heard some beautiful voice singing in it. Often himself had he heard, with indolent pleasure, there, the voice of Madame de Saint Valery —of Miss Capel's cousin.

At last the meal was over, and the whole party, having risen, prepared, as on former occasions, to take a stroll along the terraces. Hitherto Carew, when seeking to speak to Miss Consuelo Burton in private, had been content to wait till a *tête-à-tête* should arrange itself naturally ; but now, almost without any attempt at concealment, he went up to her, as she stood not far from her sisters, and said in a low voice to her :

'Will you now tell me your decision ?'

Quietly, but without hesitation, she detached herself from those near her, and slowly walked away at Carew's side into the dimness. As soon as they were well out of ear-shot and observation of the others :

'Well,' he said, 'I am waiting. Consuelo, are you going to tell me?'

'I am,' she said. 'I have thought it all over. I ought not to have taken so long in deciding. I ought not to have felt the trouble I have felt in doing so. But my mind was made up last night, after I left you—late last night; and what we have heard this afternoon in chapel has confirmed me in my decision. As to what you do, I can of course advise you only; but as to what I myself must do, I can only follow my conscience.'

'Tell me,' said Carew, 'tell me what you advise me.'

'First,' she said gently, 'let me tell you one thing. You have conveyed to me as clearly as if you had used many more words what you feel for me; and I believe you—I trust you. I—' and here her voice grew low and tremulous, 'I, if I followed my impulse, should try to make some reply to you. But why should I now? It is better not to express a feeling which most probably one will have to renounce for ever.'

'Never!' exclaimed Carew, with a sudden passionate energy. 'Consuelo, I can never renounce you. My life will be blind without you.'

'You are wrong,' she said. 'If you renounce me in the same spirit as that in which I renounce you, your blindness—if you are blinded—will be a blindness more clear than sight. Listen. I am going to speak very plainly. My advice is going to be of the most plain and practical kind. If your conduct towards the person you spoke of yesterday has been such as I understand it to have been—and I am perfectly sure I did not understand you wrongly, for women in such matters have a very quick instinct—you owe that person a debt which you are bound to pay, or at all events to offer to pay. In spite of any sacrifice it may entail on you, in spite of any loss of the power and influence that you yourself are so anxious to use for good, you are bound by honour and duty to go to her and offer yourself in marriage to her. If she accepts you, and if you act to her after your marriage as truly as you did in going back to her and marrying her, you will have chosen a higher life, even should your external influence be lessened, than you would have if, by doing a wrong to her, you had retained the power of making that influence larger.'

'And suppose,' said Carew, 'that my offer is rejected?'

'In that case,' said Miss Consuelo Burton, 'you at any rate will have done your duty. So far as she is concerned you will be free; and then, perhaps, you may find one who, though not better herself, is able to help you better. Else, else—what shall I say?—you will have made your sacrifice; and believe me, believe me in this: I too shall have made mine. Write to her, go to her. Lose no time about it; and when you know her answer, either send me your farewell, or come back to me.' Then looking at him, with a faint smile on her face, ' Do it,' she said, ' at once. Write this very night—the moment that I am gone. If you put the duty off you will persuade yourself that it is fantastic and unreal. That is the way that lives are lost and wasted. Do this duty, and you will soon see that it is real enough. It will have made a different man of you. Remember that. Now come; let us go back to the others.'

That evening, however, Carew wrote nothing. When his guests were gone he tried to compose a letter, but after a moment's attempt he pushed the paper away from him; and a little later, alone in a light boat, he was floating out on the lake, over the wavering reflections of the mountains.

The lights of Baveno were glittering at him out of the distance, and he knew that by this time Miss Consuelo Burton must be nearing them. He could not bear them. They seemed like eyes watching him. He longed to escape into the darkness and there settle his future. All of a sudden there came back into his mind Lady Chislehurst's mention at dinner of the villa of Madame de Saint Valery, and the singer's voice that issued from it. He hardly knew what impulse prompted him, but he turned the head of his boat at once in that direction, and with vigorous strokes of the oar was soon moving towards it.

Before long the Baveno lights were lost; a dark promontory had eclipsed them, then another came into sight, and another; and then a third, with the night caught in its gardens, and sprinkled through all their foliage with wavering flakes of moonlight. There were the villas, visible only by peeps, seeming to sleep softly. Their windows were dark; they meant to Carew nothing. But at last the one upon which his thoughts were centred was before him—a sudden vision; and there was something about it, something strange and startling, that at once made him stop his rowing.

There were lights in the lower windows— windows he once knew well; and, to his great surprise, these lights, which evidently came from shaded lamps, were — or at least he thought they were—of a delicate and peculiar carnation colour. It was the favourite colour of Madame de Saint Valery; and her taste seemed to have been inherited by the present occupant of the villa. The sight, as if by magic, made the past present to him. Memories rose and came hovering round him from the bosom of the lake, from the statues, from the flower-beds, from the bright interior; and he thought of the woman who, without having made him love her, had often made him wonder why she had failed to do so.

At length, rousing himself, he softly moved his oars again, and with noiseless progress advanced somewhat nearer to the shore. Presently his ears were startled, just as a moment ago his eyes had been. He heard, or thought he heard, the sound of guitar-strings stealing across the water with a faint elfin tinkle. Again he rested on his oars. He listened and watched breathlessly. He hardly knew why he did so. He hardly knew what he expected to see or hear, or for what reason it could interest him. He was rather acting in obedience to an instinctive sense that any curiosity, no matter how aimless or irrelevant, was a momentary escape from the thoughts that ought to occupy him.

Watching thus, he soon became aware that a figure of some sort had begun to move indoors, passing and repassing before the lamps. At once his pulses began to beat a little quicker, and when presently this sign of life ceased he was conscious of a strange annoying disappointment. It was as if his head were aching, and someone had ceased to press something cool against it. A moment or two later, however, his suspended excitement was renewed. Suddenly in the garden, close to the water's edge, just at the place where the shade of the trees was darkest, a small light with its arrowy rays revealed itself, and then began to move by jerks and fitfully. He recollected that at that place was the boat-house. In another moment a muffled sound reached him, like that of an oar struck accidentally against planking;

and faintly along with this came the sound of a human voice. He strained his ears with an unnecessary and blank intensity, waiting to hear more ; but meanwhile in the silence that supervened, his thoughts, like carrier pigeons, unbidden and unrestrainable, had winged their way back to Miss Consuelo Burton. The miserable realities of his situation were again finding him out. Relief, however, was at hand : again there came distraction. Perfectly clear—there could be no doubt about it—he now heard oars splashing.

His curiosity soon was supplied with even more stimulating nutriment. In another thirty seconds the darkness of trees and water gave forth a black boat into the moonlight, and in this boat there were two figures sitting. One of them seemed to be resting more or less listlessly in the stern. The other was sculling, regularly but without much vigour.

A second glance—for his first left him doubtful — revealed to Carew that they were women.

Any man who has ever felt much interest about women in general rarely loses that interest even when one of them has fixed his affections; and Carew was conscious, preoccupied as he was, of an idly sentimental curiosity in the spectacle now before him. It was not, however, of a very keen nature till he became aware as the strange boat moved in the moonlight that the hair of the woman in the stern was of the colour of pale gold.

'Good gracious!' he exclaimed to himself. 'Am I dreaming? Has this whole day been a dream? Have I slipped back eighteen months into the past?'

He was still dizzy with this helpless sort of half-doubt, when again there struck on his ears, and this time quite clearly, the twanging notes of a guitar. He recognized the shape of the instrument in the hands of the fair-haired woman; and almost before he had leisure for any further reflection a sudden thrill ran shivery down his spine; he found himself listening to that same Neapolitan hymn which Miss Capel had sung to him at Courbon-Loubet, and by which his own musicians had called her memory back to him.

Without pausing to reflect, obedient merely to an instinct, he impelled his boat rapidly towards the singer; and not thinking how singular this conduct would appear to a stranger, he very soon was gliding within a few yards of her, in the mad expectation of finding that it was Miss Capel herself. A glance told him his error. It was not Miss Capel. It was not a stranger, however: it was Madame de Saint Valery.

She at once recognised and addressed him. There was some surprise in her voice, but not much. It was the voice of one who finds, not an unexpected thing, but a thing unexpectedly soon. Carew, on the other hand, seemed completely thunderstruck.

'You!' he exclaimed at last. 'And what on earth brings you here? And back to that villa too! Who lives there? Why have you come?' Then as if this struck him as somewhat cold and uncourteous, 'Or perhaps,' he added with a smile, 'you live in the waters of the lake, and have risen up to sing in the clear moonlight. This is the second time that your voice has brought me to you.'

'My dear friend,' she said, 'why should you be so startled at seeing me? That villa is my own. I bought it not many months since; and though it is quite true that you may not have known that, still, after all, is it so very unnatural that I should be here? Do you think any special reason is necessary to account for it?' There was a faint twinkle in her eyes, as though she were gently laughing at him; but the next moment, growing quite serious, 'I will tell you plainly,' she added, 'that there is a special reason; and that reason, Mr. Carew, is this: it is my desire to see yourself. I was going to have written to you at your address in England, for when you met me at Nice, like a nice proper friend as you are, you quite forgot to tell me where you were living; but being at Milan, I saw in one of the papers that you were on the Island, or were expected there immediately, so I came here myself, and I meant to-morrow to have written to you.'

'Why,' said Carew coldly, as if he dreaded her answer, 'why do you wish to speak to me?' And as he spoke he glanced towards her companion.

'Oh,' said Madame de Saint Valery, 'don't trouble yourself about her. It's only my maid, and she speaks not a word of English. What did you think of my song—the one I was just beginning? I taught it once to a certain friend of yours, who has very likely sung it to you. But come—what I have to say will take a little time in saying. Come indoors, and I will have it out with you there.'

Carew was silent. He was regretting the whole incident. He had no inclination for a scene with Madame de Saint Valery.

'Come,' she repeated after a moment or two, with the expectant tone of a woman accustomed to be obeyed in such things.

'It is late to-night,' said Carew at last. 'No—let me come to-morrow.'

Madame de Saint Valery laid her hand on the guitar strings, and struck them all together into a clang of musical petulance.

'Stuff!' she exclaimed. 'Isn't that like a man! Since when have you kept such virtuously early hours? You are shy of me. Why are you shy? I assure you you needn't be. What I want to tell you has nothing to do with me—with me, Mr. Carew, or my wretched uninteresting life. I am not going to weary you with asking any more kindness of you. What I want to do is to do you a kindness myself. Come—please, do as I ask you. You know the boat-house. Go first; and you shall help us in landing.'

CHAPTER X.

A FEW moments more and Carew was in the carnation-coloured lamp-light, his blinking eyes straying over a wilderness of flowers and china. The air was heavy also with that odd excess of perfume with which women who are not on the best terms with the world seek to make up in their drawing-rooms for the lost ozone of respectability.

'Sit there,' said Madame de Saint Valery. 'You know the chair well. That's right; and now let me have a look at you. You are not yourself. What is it that is the matter with you ?'

'Matter?' said Carew. 'Nothing. What should be the matter ? I am only surprised at this unexpected meeting ; and your pink lamps dazzle me after the moonlight.'

'If you will not tell me,' she said, ignoring his explanation, and rising lightly from a low seat as she spoke ; 'if you will not tell me, would you like me to tell you ? I know perfectly well.'

'Tell me then,' said Carew resignedly.

'You are unhappy, my friend : that is what is the matter with you ; and here is something that will show you I know why.'

She moved to a small table covered with ornamental trifles, from amongst which she extracted a velvet case ; and then, seating herself opposite to Carew, and close to him, tapped it gently with her slim fingers. Carew, for his part, thought she must be going mad, and he remained watching her without saying a word. After a moment's pause she opened the case, and exhibited to him, on its bed of satin, a luminous pearl necklace.

'Tell me,' she said. 'Do you know what that is? It is my wedding-present for Violet Capel.'

Carew started, caught his breath, and stared at her.

'Ah,' she went on, with a slight pitying smile, 'you see I was right. Why need you try to hide it? You are unhappy because of her.'

'Perhaps,' Carew murmured, 'not in the way you think.'

'Mr. Carew,' she retorted, 'this is not friendly of you. Why are you so reserved— I might almost say so shy? Violet Capel, though her parents won't let her see me, writes to me every week. I am familiar with every thought of hers. You may trust me

that I know what I am talking about. Ah—
now you sit up and begin to show some
interest. You might, I think, have done me
that favour at first. Well, listen, and take
what I say as I mean it. I have made little
enough of my own life, God knows. I believe
I have lost, or am losing, even my sorrow at
having made so little of it. Perhaps, however, I ought to observe in passing that I am
at last on the eve of reformation and respectability. You'll hear about that some day,
and I expect when you do you'll smile. But
we won't talk about it now. What I want to
tell you is this. Whatever I may have lost,
I have not lost my sense of one thing; and
that is, my sense of the kindness you once
showed me—your real interest in my welfare.
You advised me well; you tried to make me
make the best of myself. I decided on making
the worst; but to you I am still grateful.
And now the time has come when I am able to

show my gratitude. I want to give a little saving advice to you. I am the only person, perhaps, in the whole world who could do so; and if you will listen to me it may really be for your happiness. Well, just be patient whilst I talk to you, and you will see that a bad woman may be on occasion a guide for a good man.'

'I'm not a good man,' said Carew, still moody.

'Well, no,' said his companion, 'I don't think you are.'

She laughed as she spoke, pleasantly. Carew laughed also, and he seemed in doing so to be turning into a more promising listener.

'No,' she repeated, 'you're not a good man. Still you are so-so. You are better than most of them; and you've been very good to me: that's all I care for. And now I begin again. You've admitted that your unhappiness is connected with Violet Capel. I don't think you have, by the way. But no matter, for I know that it is.'

'You are right,' said Carew. 'It is connected with her.'

'You are aware, I suppose,' Madame de Saint Valery went on, 'that Violet's marriage with the Prince de Vaucluse is arranged to take place very soon indeed?'

'Yes,' said Carew. 'I am aware, too, that she hates the man.'

Madame de Saint Valery smiled oddly and pensively. 'Violet,' she said presently, 'is a most fascinating and attractive girl; and I love her because she has always stuck to me, and still writes to me unknown to her parents, who have now forbidden her to have any communication with me. I don't wonder at any man's losing his heart to her, and a good many men have done so. But, Mr. Carew, you know very little about her. I know her through and through, and I want to explain to you just what she really is.'

'Do you know,' said Carew, with the faintest trace of pique in his voice, 'do you know the history of her acquaintance and friendship with me?'

'Hush,' said Madame de Saint Valery, 'do not interrupt me. Let me tell my story my own way; and when I have done I think you'll have cause to thank me. Well, Violet, you say, hates the Prince de Vaucluse, and will be unhappy with him. No doubt that's true; and no doubt, with her beautiful eyes looking sadly at you, she has told you so, or let you see it. Yes—she's perfectly right. He is not a man who could ever satisfy her nature. I want to tell you what her nature is. In one way she is the most innocent and ingenuous creature that ever breathed. She has done nothing that the world in its conventional language calls wrong; and she looks about her, unstung by any self-reproach, craving for some sympathy which she has never yet found. Yes, in one way you may call her virtue itself; you may call her girlish innocence itself. She doesn't, I think, know even the look of evil; and yet, for that very reason, it is in her nature to do it, and to do it as ingenuously and simply as she would do good.'

'Do you think she would,' said Carew, 'if she were once happily married, and if her desire for sympathy were satisfied?'

'What is the good,' said Madame de Saint Valery, ' of talking about "if's"? She will not be happily married. That matter is settled, and I want you thoroughly to understand that it is. I will come back to it presently; but let me go on first with what I am saying now. A year or two ago, when she and her parents were at Naples, she fell violently in love with a certain English officer who had left home for a time on account of a difference with his wife. He was a very handsome man, not far short of fifty; and many women, young girls especially, still continued to find him dangerously fascinating. Violet Capel at once took his fancy. She, for her part, in a couple of days—no, in a single evening—became infatuated about him. Mr. Carew, I am watching your face as I tell you this. I know the ways of a man's face so well; and I can see that it annoys you. I don't want to annoy you; but your annoyance is a healthy symptom.'

'I'm not annoyed,' said Carew, lying. 'Go on. This is interesting.'

'Her devotion to this man,' Madame de Saint Valery went on, 'she made no attempt to conceal. She seemed not to see anything in it that called for concealment. She was as open about it as she would have been had the object of her devotion been a bon-bon; and this very openness was the means of saving her, for her parents most judiciously at once took her away. They had another object in doing so besides saving her from one admirer; for they were very anxious that she should marry another—a sort of relation of theirs, and quite a fitting match for her. He was a man of a wholly different kind. He loved her with a tiresome religious sort of devotion, and was anxious to think her, or at any rate to make her, a saint. But though she tolerated him, and was good-natured to him, she never cared two straws for him—not even though he wrote her verses about prayer and piety: and she is devoted to poetry, and always saying scraps to herself.'

'I have seen,' murmured Carew, 'some of the very verses you speak of.'

'Poor child,' went on Madame de Saint Valery, 'it was no thanks to herself that that other man did not ruin her. She would have gone to her ruin with the same look in her eyes that most girls would have in going to their Confirmation. Listen, Mr. Carew : this describes her exactly. She has all the heart of Eve after the fall, and all the conscience of Eve untouched in Paradise.'

'Then there is the more reason,' said Carew sadly, ' why someone who can guide her wisely should be with her to guide her always.'

'Again you interrupt me,' said Madame de Saint Valery. 'What I have to tell you is only half finished. I have described to you only one side of her character. I have described to you the way in which passion or love appeals to her, and the way in which she responds to it. I must now describe her to you in relation to the world and worldliness.'

'Worldliness !' exclaimed Carew. 'She hardly knows what the word means.'

'That shows,' said Madame de Saint Valery, 'how easily you men are deceived. Violet is affected by the world very much as she is affected by love—with the same mixture of ingenuousness and what good people call evil. She appreciates worldly distinction, I must tell you, with a wonderful quickness, though not always, I dare say, with correctness. The brilliancy of a great position, however vaguely she conceives it, attracts her exactly as some pretty thing attracts a child, or as some man she might be in love with would attract her. The only difference would be this: just as she would cling to the man with the ingenuous passion I spoke of, so would she cling to worldly position with an equally ingenuous obstinacy; and this obstinacy, if it came into conflict with that passion, would have a noiseless and almost unacknowledged, but still a complete, victory over it. She herself would not realize what the process was, and for the simple reason that she would not look at it. She would think she was the victim of circumstances; she would softly and sadly pity herself. And yet if anyone suggested to her she could make the circumstances different he would find she stuck to them as a snail sticks to its shell.'

'But, surely,' interposed Carew, 'the man she was in love with at Naples—there was no worldliness in the case of her fondness for him?'

'You see,' said Madame de Saint Valery, 'she was only beginning then. And besides, I don't think I told you what that man did. The morning before the Capels left Naples, he, seeing that Violet was going to escape his clutches, went off to Venice with an opera-dancer. Violet Capel is still tender over his memory, and his infidelity still fills her heart with a feeling that has every resemblance to a profound sorrow, except that somehow it does not seem to pain her. Well, by-and-by, at Paris, the Prince de Vaucluse met her. You know what he is—one of the most dissolute men in Europe, and, apart from a certain superficial knowledge of the world, one of the silliest. But then, of course, he is immensely rich: his horses win races, and he gives dinners to royalty. The Prince de Vaucluse at once fell in love with Violet, and his love had all that folly of which only a middle-aged man of the world is capable. I don't know which to say she was—his passion or his whim. Anyhow, a week after he had first seen her, he made her an offer of marriage. Violet was flattered by the offer, and dazzled by it, and, imagining that her heart was for ever buried at Naples, she at once accepted him. Her mother did all she could in opposition to the engagement, and the General, for various reasons, insisted on a considerable delay before the marriage. As to this last point Violet was quite submissive. She was rather pleased, indeed, at having her doom deferred; but she was fully decided that it neither could nor should be altered. Her future, to her own mind, was finally settled, and the prospect from that moment became the foundation of her thoughts—not of her happy thoughts only, but of her soft melancholy also. Well, Mr. Carew, by-and-by she fell in love with you. The details of that process you know better than I do. Still, I know something, and I can at any rate tell you this—for you mustn't think Violet worse or more heartless than she is. No, in her way she is all heart. Whatever she seemed to feel for you she did feel. Your presence, your personality, as it were mesmerized her; and all that tender music—tender, imploring, unsatisfied, full of far-away longings which her whole being seemed to make under your influence—that, Mr. Carew, is the real music of her nature. It is as real as the sound the wind makes on an æolian harp. But for all that it hasn't altered her conduct. It has not made her seriously even dream of doing so. Look at this,' Madame de Saint Valery continued. ' Here is a letter which I had from her only three days ago.' And she put a letter into Carew's hands.

'My darling,' it ran—

' Yes, the time will now soon come when I shall belong wholly to him. I mean, as wholly as I can ever belong to anybody. Ah me! no doubt it is all for the best; and yet once or twice it was a very hard struggle, when Mr. Carew, if I would only have let him—— But why talk of that? Bygones had best be bygones. His way and mine lie down different channels, though surely they are channels which one day will re-unite us as friends.

' And now, darling, tell me—have you been to see the woman about my pocket-handkerchiefs? I want, if you remember, five dozen of them, with the monogram V. de V., and the coronet above it. They are to be done in five different colours—one dozen of each. The two V.'s ought to be very pretty. As to my pale-green silk, I have acted on your suggestion, and the train is to be rather shorter. Nearly all my trousseau is being made at Nice; and you were quite right—it could hardly have been done better in Paris. I have done, too, what you advised about my dress-improver. I agree with you, it is much better. By the way, your hands are the same size as mine, and exactly the same shape. If you want any gloves, you should write at once to Lang—I mean Lang at Nice. He has some that would fit you even better than any you could have made for you—*gants de Suède*, with from eight to fourteen buttons.

'*A propos* of the shops at Nice, there is some lovely tapestry at a place in the Avenue de la Gare, which I shall make the Prince buy for my boudoir in Paris. I told you I had decided in November on having it quite done up. You too, when you are married, will settle again in Paris. God bless you, darling. You must get a house near ours.

'I am very busy—I have so much to do and think about. The dressmaker is here nearly every hour of the day ; and mamma fusses so, and I have so little time to write. But I must say one thing more. Have you secured Eugène for us ? I trust you have. The Prince says he is a far better courier than Cirio ; and after our marriage we are to travel for two whole months, and then be in England in time for a London ball or two, and for Goodwood. The travelling—think how delicious! You know how I love travelling —I don't mean with mamma and the General, who are always at me about something ; but now, when I shall be my own mistress, able to come and go as I like, and ask people I like to dinner. But I must stop. "Violet, Violet." That's mamma calling. "You must come up," she is saying, "to try on this new body again. Come instantly." And I must come. Good-bye!

'Your own
'Violet.'

Madame de Saint Valery waited till Carew had finished his reading, and she allowed him to ruminate over it for a little while in silence.

At last she said, 'Are you quite convinced now? And do you see why I have been so anxious—as a true friend—to speak to you? I know you love Violet. I know she is just the girl to make a man unhappy; and you have probably still hopes of persuading her to alter her purpose. Should you attempt to do this you would merely distress her uselessly. I think you might make as much impression as that—distress her and mortify yourself; and I wished, since an opportunity offered, to convince you of two things : one, that you have no hope of making her your wife ; and the other, that she would not be a wife really worthy of you. I love her myself; but you deserve someone better, or someone, shall I say, different.'

Carew, during the reading of Miss Capel's pages, had experienced a mixture of the most oddly-conflicting emotions. He compared this letter with the one she had so lately written to him, and he felt himself stung by the distinct poison of jealousy, whilst a mad longing, unreal as he knew it to be, once more thrilled through him to make the writer his own. Conscience, too, with added animation, was pricking the sides of his intent ; and yet at the same time a glow of unexpected happiness was flooding his mind—indeed, was almost overwhelming it—as he came to understand what was really the situation.

His feelings found expression, or rather a natural mask for themselves, in the blank stare which he fixed on Madame de Saint Valery. She could not understand it. When at last he spoke he dared hardly to trust his voice. He put the utmost restraint on its inflexion, and this only seemed to perplex Madame de Saint Valery more. To her ears it came like the voice of sheer desperation.

'If,' he said, 'I were to ask her to marry me now, do you mean solemnly to tell me that there is no chance of her accepting me—that there is none if I went to her, if I told her I had a home ready for her, and would take her off to it immediately?'

'There is no chance,' said Madame de Saint Valery, 'absolutely none.'

'How can you know this?' said Carew. 'It is impossible that you can be certain of it. Nothing but certainty will prevent my going to her to-morrow. That is my resolution, and God knows I have not made it lightly.'

'Then, in that case,' said Madame de Saint Valery, 'I can give you certainty. Violet Capel is married to the Prince already. Don't start. I should have preferred to conceal the fact; but what you have said has forced me to let you know it. They were together in London early this year, and I was there. I knew what the Prince was. I knew how strong his whims—we will call them whims, it is a prettier word than the right one—I knew how strong his whims were, and how capricious. My fear was that he might satisfy his whim for Violet, and then get tired of his whim for marrying her. Mrs. Capel would not hear of the marrying being done then; and this delay has so increased the Prince's keenness that he urged the girl to marry him privately before the Registrar. She made me her confidante, and I approved of the plan.

The marriage took place one morning, and I was present. But now, Mr. Carew, mark this—I pledge you my word it's true: as soon as the ceremony—I mean, the formality—was over, I did just what I had arranged to do. I took Violet back with me to her people, keeping the transaction a profound secret; and I made the Prince understand that, for various good reasons, he will not be able to call his bride his own till he claims her openly and marries her in his own country. As for Violet, she hardly realizes what has been done. She knows she is married, but her imagination has never grasped the fact.'

Carew, in a tone that filled Madame de Saint Valery with astonishment, exclaimed several times, 'Can this really be true!' Then, rising from his seat, he paced up and down the room, avoiding the furniture with slightly impatient gestures, once or twice muttering something to himself, but uttering nothing intelligible to his companion. At last, pausing in front of her, a smile broke over his face, and holding out his hand to her, he exclaimed with suppressed enthusiasm, ' God bless you! A thousand times God bless you! I thank you more than you can even imagine or dream of.'

Madame de Saint Valery stared at him in bewilderment. He seemed to understand her expression.

' You think me odd,' he said. ' No doubt you do. Indeed, of course, you do. I will explain it all to-morrow. I can explain nothing to-night. You have so completely astonished me that I really can hardly tell which I am doing—standing on my head or my heels. Let me go. Again, a thousand times thank you.' And offering his hand to her, he prepared to move towards the window.

' Don't forget,' she said, and she looked

up at him as if appealing for kindness—
'don't forget to come back to me and to tell
me all about yourself. I too have something to tell you about my own future.'

'Yes, yes,' said Carew, with a sort of
absent eagerness. 'Your own future—tell
me about that. Tell me all. You are going
to be happy, I hope.'

'I will see you down to your boat,' said
Madame de Saint Valery, and you shall hear
this unimportant piece of news by the way.
I,' she went on presently, as they emerged
from the window, 'am going shortly to
become a respectable woman—that is to
say, as respectable as circumstances will permit of. I don't know '—and she gave a little
hard laugh, ' that this respectability includes
much respect from myself. I am going to
be married—married to an Englishman. I
don't pretend to love him, but I like him,
though other people laugh at him ; and I

shall, I think, be pretty well able to manage him. Anyhow, considering what for two months—for two months only—my life was at Nice this winter, my life with him will be comparative peace and happiness.'

'And who is the man?' Carew asked.

'Let me see. Shall I tell you?' she said. 'No, I think not to-night. I am somewhat shy of doing so. Wait—let me go back to the drawing-room, and I will bring you something which will explain the whole affair to you.'

In a minute or so she returned with a newspaper, which she put into Carew's hand; and when he had taken it she then gave him a letter.

'When you get home,' she said, 'look at both. You will then know the history. The letter is written from a friend of yours to a friend of mine. You will agree that my friend has given me the best test of his friendship in sending me the most disagreeable things that other people can say about me. I am glad, too, that you should know the worst. It's not bad. You will only think it contemptible; and when you know it, try still to keep a kind thought for me. Good-night, and give me your congratulations.'

CHAPTER XI.

AN hour or so later Carew was in his own room again. The blank sheet of note-paper which he had so lately tried to fill, and tried in vain, still lay on the blotting-book. Now he seized his pen, which had then refused obstinately to so much as make a beginning with the name of Violet Capel. He seized his pen, and began writing rapidly. The first word of his letter was not 'Violet,' but 'Consuelo.'

When he had finished he looked at his watch. It was half-past three in the morning. He remembered, with a pang of conscience, that his servant must be sitting up for him. He tinkled a hand-bell; the man appeared, blinking; and Carew told him to go to bed, leaving a door to the garden open. Before long, unable to sleep or rest, he had glided out again into the chilly and fresh night air; and again seeking his boat, he rowed across to Baveno.

The hotel where his friends were staying was dark in all its windows, and the doors were closed. But he was not in a mood to think too much about trifles, and after a great knocking and ringing he managed to wake the *concierge*. The man, when he appeared, not unnaturally was not in complete possession of his clothes, his wits, or his temper; but an immediate apology and the tender of a seductive coin restored him to his customary senses, and to something of his customary civility, and he received from Carew's hands an envelope addressed to Miss Consuelo Burton, which he engaged should be sent up to her the very first thing in the morning. It was superscribed *Immediate* ; and Carew had but few doubts that no needless time would elapse before he received an answer.

And now re-embarking, a feeling of sudden vigour seemed to infuse itself into his muscles, and for the first time since his new prospects had dawned on him did the full sense of his happiness really come to him, filling all his spirit, and disturbing it with a limitless exhilaration. The condition of his mind seemed to communicate itself to his oars, and tingle through them to the blades as they met the water. Not to the Island did Carew turn the prow, but hither and thither in aimless and wandering courses did he restlessly row himself over the sheets of the starlit lake. Great happiness, like great sorrow, will not at first suffer us to look it in the face ; and his spirit confided its secret to his muscles and his nerves before it was calm enough to confide it entirely to itself.

At last, having followed an eastward course for some time, he put his boat about, with thoughts of returning home ; and there, as he turned, far off behind the spikes of the mountains, he saw that the sky was pale with the first colours of dawn. There, too, was the star of the morning shining, bright with a trembling steadfastness ; and Carew felt that for him a star had arisen also.

He did not cease rowing, but his stroke became slower and less excited. On his spirit there descended the solemn hush of the daybreak, which makes all the earth seem like some holy sanctuary : and there came back to him two lines of Goethe's :

> The woman-soul leadeth us
> Upward and on.

The lines came back to him, and remained fixed in his consciousness.

Meanwhile, on the sliding and glassy waves, that moved to left and right at the touch of his dipping oars, there began to flicker a gleam of faint saffron and rose-colour; and the breeze of the morning laid its first breath on his cheek, and gently touched a straying lock of his hair.

'Now for me,' he said to himself, as he gradually neared the Island, 'now begins the day, and not the moonlight—the day of labour and action, of weariness, of disappointment—the day that follows the hush of the hopeful morning; but hope, with her to guide me, will live through every failure, and she will always make a perpetual morning in my heart.'

The granite steps of the landing-stage were thick with dew when he reached them. The few lights of Baveno, though still bright, looked belated, and the mounting saffron was faint in the dome over him. Having moored his boat, he still stood by the water, looking across to the spot where the heart that was his was beating; and thoughts thronged on his mind of many careers and labours to which his life, with hers, might be dedicated. Visions also, though he knew them too bright for truth, floated before him and made his being tingle—visions of great works done amongst the toiling masses, of comfort and health invading the fastnesses of degradation, and the fire of faith once more shining on eyeballs long blind to it. The feud of classes he seemed to see dying, and trust and duty replacing them like a new religion. Meanwhile, in the actual world around him the morning breeze had by this time subsided;

> And east and west, without a breath,
> Mixed their twin lights, like life and death,
> To broaden into boundless day.

At length a weariness, settling like dew upon his eyelids, warned him to think of rest; but just as he was turning, his hand touched one of his pockets, and he recollected that in it were Madame de Saint Valery's documents—the letter and the newspaper.

It was light enough now to read, and with a whimsical access of curiosity he drew them out and inspected them. He opened the letter first. He at once knew the handwriting. To his surprise, it was that of Lord Stonehouse. The letter was to Prince Olgorouki.

'My dear Olgorouki,' it ran. 'If you are as great an admirer as you used to be of that beautiful Comtesse de Saint Valery, whom I unfortunately have not the honour of knowing—if you are as great an admirer of her now as you were in those days at Nice when she was so much taken up with an illustrious compatriot of yours, you will perhaps be amused to hear something about this *magnifico* she is engaged to marry. For certain reasons, which when he meets you next he will doubtless be delighted to inform you of, he has lost, so he thinks, in the eyes of the London world something of that fashionable splendour with which his own imagination had invested him; so now, like a man of infinite resource as he is, his hopes and attentions are turned on *le high-life* of the Continent. Well, there is really a sort of genius in the stroke, not because it aims so high, but because it does not aim too high. Having learnt that Madame de Saint Valery's cousin is going to marry that odious Prince de Vaucluse, he has hit on the idea of marrying himself to the cousin of a live princess. Indeed, the Prince and he are such a pair of snobs and impostors that, upon my word, they will not pull badly together; and in Paris, no doubt, he will from time to time still find some impecunious peer to dine with him. I think, my dear fellow, all this will amuse you, because you know at Nice how jealous you used to be of him, and how angry he was when he found our friend Carew talking to the lady under the garden wall. I shrewdly imagine that the bridegroom that is to be was hardly aware then of the fineness of his own character, and how little it would take to make his intentions strictly honourable. There is only one blow in store for him, and that is too tragical. His wife will be unable in France to retain her title, and, though the cousin of a live princess, she will only be Mrs. Inigo.'

Carew was conscious of an almost incredulous smile, and then turned to the paper. Having shaken the leaves open, he at length saw the following passage :

' A marriage is arranged, and will shortly take place, between Geoffry Inigo, Esq., of 50 Halkin Street, and of the Turf, White's, Marlborough, and Carlton Clubs, and Élise,

Comtesse de Saint Valery, widow of the late Comte de Saint Valery, so long renowned in the diplomatic circles of Europe. An unusual interest attaches itself to this alliance from the distinguished position of both the parties concerned, the bride-elect being about shortly to become by marriage the cousin of the Prince de Vaucluse. The wedding, which will take place at the English Embassy at Paris, will, it is expected, be of the most brilliant description, most of the representatives of foreign Courts having had invitations sent to them. The Prince de Vaucluse will probably give the bride away.'

One thing had struck Carew faintly the moment he discovered this paragraph. It was not in that part of the paper usually devoted to such announcements, and when he came to the end of it an audible laugh broke from him. Owing to some carelessness, some mistake, or a sense of humour in some quarter of the editorial bureau, at the end of the paragraph, in brackets, came the fatal word '[Advertisement].'

A smile was still on his lips as he slowly reverted to the house, but the solemn hopes and happiness which he trusted might last a life-time were not disturbed, and did not even seem incongruous as the twinkling light gleamed on it, of one of life's least absurdities.

THE END.

G. & C.

PRINTED BY
SPOTTISWOODE AND CO., NEW-STREET SQUARE
LONDON

www.ingramcontent.com/pod-product-compliance
Lightning Source LLC
Chambersburg PA
CBHW030310240426
43673CB00040B/1124